OPENING
to CONSCIOUSNESS *with*
RELATIONSHIP RIDING

Barbra-Ann King

ISBN: 978-0-9813173-0-4

Published by:
Hoof Print Publishing, November 2009
Layout, Design & Printing: Really Small Vernon Press,
www.rsvp.bc.ca

Photo Credits:
Cover photo: John Hall
All photos except chapters 2 and 10: Hoof Print Publishing
Photos chapter 2 and 10: Louise Bolduc

Disclaimer:
This book is intended to provide information only. The author and/or publisher will not be liable or responsible for any loss or damage caused directly or indirectly by the use or attempted use of any information in this book.

"Progress is impossible without change, and those who cannot change their minds cannot change anything."

- George Bernard Shaw

ACKNOWLEDGEMENTS

Writing a book is a long, solitary journey and I enjoyed it every step of the way. But I would not have been able to do it without the love and support of my family and friends.

To my husband, Aeron, thanks for giving me back my wings and allowing me to fly again. Your love, support and trust in me and my work makes everything so much easier. Thanks for believing in me.

To my daughter, Kassia, thanks for coming along with me on this wonderful journey, putting aside a conventional upbringing to embrace magic and horses. Your support and love mean the world to me.

To Aeron, Sandra-Marie, Helen and Marcia for helping out in the editing process. Thanks for your time, comments and wisdom!

This book was written to answer the demand of students and clients of Relationship Riding. Thank you all for encouraging me to "write it all down" and patiently waiting for the finished product.

To all horse owners/lovers that took a leap of faith and jumped on the Relationship Riding journey, Thank You! Together, we *will* make a difference in the lives of horses as we enrich our own in the process.

To Dad, for believing in me ... always!

TABLE OF CONTENTS

PREFACE

"Questioning and exploring are the first steps towards change."

- Barbara Coloroso

"All truth passes through three stages:
First, it is ridiculed;
Second, it is violently opposed; and
Third, it is accepted as self-evident."

- Arthur Schopenhauer

Many horse trainers get a big "a-ha" moment during their careers that changes their lives. It asks of them to re-evaluate the way they have been handling horses and this awakening forces them to see if they have what it takes to move away from the old, traditional methods they have been using in order to follow a new path and way of thinking.

My story is no different. My "a-ha" moments came in small increments and once I understood them well and implemented them in my teaching, new "a-ha" moments, or teachings, would come to me ... and they still do to this day.

Some of my accounts in this book do not paint a pretty picture of mankind in regards to horses. I do not wish to offend anyone in doing so, I just want us, as human animals, to open up to other forms of consciousness in order to become a better specie for the well-being of our environment, planet and each other. If you find my propos offending, you might be resisting what you've known all along. That's a very good sign! It means you're on the right track of awareness towards your actions and ways of doing things. I use the terms "him" and "her", referring to the horse's gender, interchangeably throughout the book. I enjoy interacting with stallions, geldings, mares, yearlings and foals and have no preference regarding their gender.

Throughout the book I reiterate points that need to be emphasized because of their importance. If you notice the repetition, please pay special attention.

This is the story of Relationship Riding and how this knowledge came to me. Horse wisdom has enriched my life in ways I am only beginning to understand. Horses will always be my best teachers and friends.

Barbra-Ann King
Founder of the Relationship Riding technique

1

"The important thing about choosing a path in life isn't about where you are going, but who you take along with you".

- Unknown

Photo courtesy Hoof Print Publishing

D efinition of Relationship Riding: *Bringing ancient equine teachings to a modern world while challenging conventional methods.*

A long time ago, circa 11th-13th century, warriors on horseback hit the battlefields. Their trusted mounts were stallions, as they had more stamina and courage than mares which were mainly used for breeding. These warriors were fully armoured, holding a shield in one hand and a sword in the other. They rode bareback and bridle less. Together horse and rider confronted the enemy, stopping and going on command, moving right and left, backing up, rearing up, and do-ing some amazing moves to conquer the enemy (these moves are still performed today by the famous Lipizzaner stallions, but under differ-ent circumstances). The warrior protected himself with his shield as he warded off assailants that tried to harm him or, more commonly, his stallion in order to dismount the rider. While holding his shield and sword, the mounted warrior had no means of directing his horse with a bit and bridle. All communication between horse and rider was done through the body, heart and soul. So much so that when a young man was chosen to become a knight, he knew he would become a dif-ferent man, one that would be in touch with his true self, in order to have this very deep and authentic relationship with his horse.

Over the centuries we have stopped going to battle with horses. We used them as transportation needs (horse power) for farming the fields and travelling. Then, horses became a means of recreation, which entailed a different type of exploitation.

Today horses are mainly used as recreation. Treed saddles were necessary to carry heavy equipment across battlefields and a variety of bits and bridles were introduced to have more control over horses as well as immediate response. Stallions stopped running freely with mares and foals and suddenly man became an expert in knowing what a horse needs including dressing them up when the weather is not cooperating, having them wear shoes and making them live in houses with a roof over their heads and an un-natural heat source. That's when horses stopped having an extraordinary relationship with their owners based on trust, honesty and love. Instead, they started serving mankind's ego. The dominating approach took over and with it came cruel methods of handling and exploitation. Today we can no longer look at the horse as being a free spirited wild animal that loves to move, play and interact socially. They are regularly hunted and killed in Canada.

The era of natural horsemanship showed up slowly, taking over the horse world as it is known today. One "whisperer" after another explained to the rest of the equestrian world how it isn't necessary to be "rough" with a horse in order to have him "obey" you. Although each of these natural horsemen "personas" have their own unique approach and ideas (tricks?) in the techniques they use, the foundation for their work is all the same: make the wrong answer difficult or uncomfortable for the horse and the right answer easy. This is better known as negative reinforcement and these methods dominate the world of horses today. Whether it is on a competitive basis or for recreational purposes, horses are responding to their owners/handlers out of either fear, pain or discomfort (sometimes all three).

In the book "The Art of Horsemanship" written twenty-three centuries ago by Xenophon, his message is clear that horses never need to be anything else but gentled.

If we look back at our warriors riding their trusted stallions to battle in the 11th-13th century, none of these horses "obeyed" their riders because of negative reinforcement. There was a much deeper "training method" used where a horse responded out of willingness.

Today's horses are no different than the specie from that era. Today it is still possible to connect with our horses in the same manner the mounted warriors did, bitless, treeless and barefeet.

This book is meant to explain how it was done then and how to apply this technique to every equestrian discipline today. This book will explain how to have a horse respond to you out of willingness, not fear, pain or discomfort. Although a lot of research and personal experience back up what is written, the horses themselves offered their knowledge and experience, telling me what they want humans to know about them via telepathy. So, if you wonder how I can possibly know about some of the things you are about to read, keep in mind there are thousands of years of knowledge and experience cantering our fields and that are graciously offering this information for the benefit of all.

As you read this book, the information presented will either resonate with you, or not. If not, it simply means that you are at a stage in your life where you are not ready to embark on this journey. That being said, if you picked up this book with the intention of reading it, or even out of curiosity, you will most probably come across information that is pertinent to you in your journey with horses. These may be your first baby steps on your journey to rediscovering the equine world, and rediscovering your authentic self in the process.

No matter where this journey takes you, may it be filled with joy and eye-opening adventures to enhance your life. I truly believe horses make us better human beings.

Now, turn the page and start your journey!

THE HEALING TOUCH OF HORSES

2

"The essential joy of being with horses is that it brings us in contact with rare elements of grace, beauty, spirit and fire!"

- Oliver Wendall Holmes

Photo courtesy Louise Bolduc

Have you ever asked yourself why you enjoy touching horses so much? Is it the warmth emanating from their bodies? Or maybe their soft coat? There's something about touching a horse that makes us feel really good. Maybe it's because we finally mustered up the courage to get close enough to touch one! Our hands are drawn to the horse like a powerful magnet that we can't resist. What is this powerful energy that takes over us and makes it irresistible?

Horses have tremendous healing energy and as energetic beings ourselves we are drawn to this vibrating frequency. Have you noticed how we automatically put our hands over a wound or pain anywhere on our bodies when it hurts? Even on other people's bodies we do this, especially on children. When a child bumps their head, we automatically cover it up with our hands, after removing theirs!

Many thousands of years ago, when humans had not veered away from their natural abilities to heal, they possessed healing energy that emanated mostly from their hands. Our bodies still know that. Furthermore our bodies also know that we still possess this healing energy. All of us do. That's why we have an automatic reaction of putting our hands where it hurts. The good news is, we can all rekindle this healing energy from within and use it on ourselves as well as others. It is also very enjoyable to use it on cats, dogs, horses and any other pet you may have.

When we are urged to touch a horse, we are simply connecting with another source of healing energy, one that can heal our soul. This powerful energy attracts us and when we touch a horse, something inside us quiets and we feel very peaceful. Mind you, in order to feel this, you have to have a clear mind and be in the moment. When we are busy thinking about a hundred things a minute, outer knowledge and experiences cannot enter our minds and guide us towards extraordinary inner experiences. These are known as channels, thoughts, or knowings.

The next time you walk up to a horse and have an urge to touch them, think about this and take a minute to clear your mind completely. Make it a more valuable experience by imagining that you are touching a horse for the first time. As you awaken your senses you will create awareness within yourself and open up your channel to receiving messages, guidance and knowledge from the Spirit of the Horse.

This will also encourage you to be in the moment, the way horses live. They are not internally wired to wonder about what awaits them later (thoughts of the future) nor dwell on what happened a few hours ago (thoughts of the past, although they do have memories). Their survival skills keep them in the "now", the present moment, in order to be aware of their surroundings and survive any approaching danger. Predators can creep up on them at anytime and if they are lost in thought, they might end up being somebody's lunch. As human beings, we constantly think about everything else in our life except being in the present moment. Eckart Tolle wrote a wonderful book about being in the moment entitled "The Power of Now". And if you think about it for a minute, there really is no other moment that exists except the present one. In the present moment we don't have to worry about later, tomorrow, yesterday, the past, etc. The present moment is perfect, peaceful and fun to be in. It does take a little practice to stay in the moment, but it will rapidly become second nature to you.

When working with horses, it is very important that you be fully present and in the moment. Not only will you benefit from their healing energy that will calm and sooth your soul, you will also be aware of what they are telling you at all times (Yes! They are constantly talking to us!). By being aware you won't ignore the small signs in their behaviour that could very well end up being disastrous if not addressed now. We often hear horse owners say "I didn't see it coming at all! He just bucked me off out of the blue!" In reality, horses do not buck us off out of the blue. They try to tell us in many ways that something is wrong before actually bucking. Because we are not in the moment and we do not understand their language, we miss out on this communication and the end result is usually not something we expected.

Another important factor about being present has to do with us being their leader. We often "check out" when riding horses on a beautiful, scenic trail ride. We are busy yapping with friends, or worse, yapping on a cell phone, looking at the scenery and not paying any attention to our mount. Horses see this as being left to fend for themselves so they decide to take over leadership and make their own decisions about where to go and at what speed. If they feel vulnerable because of the lack of leadership on your part, they will spook at the rustling bushes and may dump you before running back to the barn, because in their mind you are an uncooperative burden holding them back from being eaten by the monster residing in the bushes. On the other hand, being in the moment lets them know that you are still doing your job as a leader and you are fully aware of your surroundings. Keep in mind that horses communicate through telepathy and they can read your mind very well. I can hear some of you commenting already, "Barbra-Ann, when I go on a trail ride I want to enjoy the scenery and relax. That's why I trail ride in the first place." My answer to that is simple. When you are driving the panoramic road to your destination, do you totally check out and risk running over everything that crosses your path? No. Somehow you manage to have a "soft mind" and while you are taking in all the breathtaking scenery, you are still totally aware of the road and what speed you are driving at. It is no different when you ride your horse.

A horse's nature is one of giving, tolerance and kindness which all contribute to the healing they give us when we are in contact with them. They look for those qualities in us also and together we exchange some powerful healing and knowledge that enriches our friendship and relationship. For those who think that you don't need all this healing, think again. Healing affects us on various levels and unless we are enlightened, we all need to learn about unconditional love.

This journey with horses has led me to experience fabulous lessons and teachings. My commitment to the Relationship Riding technique has been tested time and time again. Sometimes it was very subtle and required me to rethink long and hard how I was going to do something before proceeding to accept or reject the idea. Every time an opportunity came up, if I wasn't in the moment I would have missed the "teachings" or I would have made the wrong decision, leading to grave mistakes. Here is a good example of this. Hawk is a rescued Morgan gelding, approximately 12 years old. After owning him for well over one year, he still had me confused and often frustrated. By now, I could tell he had been physically abused. I am very grateful to the man that saw him at the feedlot and decided to give him a second chance. I spent many months handling him gently but still I couldn't get a farrier near him without having him tranquilized. Because Hawk is a survivor, having been stolen, gelded, abandoned, etc., he resisted the tranquilizers which meant he needed double doses. After a while, the vet couldn't approach him either.

One day, I met a very experienced farrier that trimmed hooves the natural way. Because all of my horses are bare feet year round, I decided to give this farrier a try. His approach to trimming made sense to me and, as a certified Equine Body Worker, I've learned a few things about trimming hooves. This farrier did a good job and was so experienced at handling horses, I asked him how he would handle a horse like Hawk, who badly needed his hooves trimmed by now. The farrier told me about the nerve line technique. I had never heard about this technique but he said it was gentle and very effective and he had been using it himself for more than forty years. He then proceeded to explain how a soft cotton rope was placed behind the horses ears, at the poll, where sensitive nerves run. He then cleverly wrapped the rest of the rope around the horse's head to fit like a halter, with the remaining rope hanging from it. He then taught the horse the meaning of the word "whoa": when the horse moved around or refused to have his feet handled, the farrier would simply say "whoa". If the horse continued to misbehave, the farrier spoke louder and said "whoa" again and again a little louder still if that didn't work. After three "whoas" and no success, he then tugged hard on the rope which created an instant shock behind the horse's ears. He then very quickly released the rope, saying that usually one good tug was enough, that the horses responded pretty quickly to standing still when he said "whoa" after that.

At first, I thought about how horses kick each other in the field when things are not right and I figured this technique was not any worse. If the horse didn't listen to his leader, there had to be a consequence, thus the rope tugging. But, something inside of me resisted and I still didn't feel good about having this done to Hawk. I needed to think about this some more before continuing.

Then, I got into the horse's "shoes" so to speak and thought about why they moved around or refused to have their feet handled in the first place. The answer was quite simple: they didn't trust the human wanting to handle them. Was I going to create pain, fear, and/or discomfort to Hawk because he was scared and untrusting or was I going to stick to what I believe in and get him to respond to me out of willingness. The answer came to me quite clearly. Willingness is the only answer!

Out in the herd, when horses kick or bite each other, it is always because one of them has pushed their boundaries and disrespected the other. That merits a strong correction because horses must protect their personal boundaries in order to be respected by the other herd members (more on boundaries in the chapter entitled The Zone). But horses do not hurt each other simply because one doesn't trust the other and won't do what he's told (dominating attitude). Horses know they have to earn each other's trust and they don't put such demands on each other.

My dilemma was solved. I wasn't going to create pain and discomfort to a horse that had been badly abused physically which gave him every reason not to trust humans in the first place. Instead, I decided to act like a lead horse and push him out of the two-horse herd we created every time he moved around. This showed him that he was free to move away from this uncomfortable situation if he needed to. It also showed him that I had the qualities of a good leader, i.e. besides being able to move him around I stayed calm and didn't get emotional, my vibrations and energy stayed at the same level which was non-threatening to him. Within no time, I was picking up all four feet and Hawk was standing still. He just needed to know that he was free to move if he needed to but because he felt safe with me, he chose to stand still, knowing that I would be his protector, just like a good equine leader would do for him.

Because I took the time to understand and accept Hawk as he is, allowing him to move through his fears at his own pace, our relationship grew stronger and we started trusting each other entirely.

I believe that healing in itself has no agenda and that the healing process is different for each individual. When healing takes place in a safe and nurturing environment, the process happens faster and the results last longer, maybe even a lifetime.

Healing is a journey, not an end result. Once an issue or situation is "healed", it doesn't mean that this issue won't show up again at a later time under different circumstances.

COMMUNICATION BETWEEN MAN AND EQUINE

3

*"When we listen to our horses, we get an education.
When we don't, we get an experience."*

- Mark Rashid

Photo courtesy Hoof Print Publishing

C ommunicating with horses is complex. Horses have abilities that humans no longer use in communicating, and vice versa (i.e. telepathy).

We know horses use extra-sensory perception but it is only one of the aspects of their communication vessels. They also use telepathy and are experts at body language. Combined, these three ways of communicating make up a very complex language.

Man's language is also complex in some ways. We use some extra-sensory perception, some body language and hardly any telepathy anymore, although there are numerous anecdotal instances noted by nearly everyone I talk to of telepathic experiences such as knowing of impending bad news. Man relies mainly on verbal language. It is quick and relays ideas from the brain with no perceptible delay, although, the accuracy of the message transmitted is questionable. Verbal language is not always accurate for transmitting messages, especially when communicating between different species (i.e. man vs dog, man vs horses, man vs woman!). There are too many variables to make this method 100% fool-proof: cultural differences and use of expressions, accents, terminology, etc.

Based on spiritual communications I have had with ancestor horse spirits, horses have been waiting for mankind to evolve to a higher level of consciousness for a long time in order to communicate with them on a more accurate basis, using telepathy, vibrational energy and body language. Meanwhile, equines have been playing the role that humans have imposed on them (sport horses, work horses and pleasure horses for the most part). Communication then becomes one way, no matter how much humans say they understand what their horses want. Unless humans can actually feel, hear, "know" what their horses are saying, they are not communicating with them. Humans only understand what they want to. For example, we shave off their long winter coats and cover them up in blankets to keep them warm, all because we think this is best for them. But do we truly and honestly care what our horses think about all this, or is the fact that we only have two hours to spare with our horse and we have a scheduled riding lesson that takes up half that time, have a role to play in all of this? If the horse's long winter coat is shaved, we won't have to spend an hour drying them off after riding them in a heated indoor arena. Somehow, we manage to convince ourselves that we love our horses and are doing this for them.

In our quest to get closer to horses and to enhance our communication with them, human beings try everything imaginable to please them. We touch them where we think they want to be touched, we rub them like we think it feels good to them and we do all of this hoping our horses understand that we just want to be kind to them. Besides having "predatorial" behaviour, human beings are first and foremost primates. This means we touch, grab, hit, etc. using our hands. It is necessary to have an understanding of how to respect a horse's personal space, but let's not kid ourselves, horses know exactly what we are feeling and thinking when we approach them and what our ulterior motives are. They also know if we are on a higher level of consciousness, open to learning and listening to what they have to share with us. As humans, we sometimes have a harder time recognizing that we are more than physical beings. Like any other living creature, humans also have a higher self, a soul, an inner self. Only, horses seem to be better connected to their higher power and source of knowledge than we are. So, they are in a better position to recognize us when we "connect" to our inner self than we think they are capable of. Most horse owners/lovers who have spent enough time with these animals will have some kind of extraordinary experience to tell. Whether they have heard a horse's voice, felt that the horse was staring at them directly in the eyes, have experienced without a doubt that the horse knew what they were thinking, horse lovers across the world will have a story to tell. If humans allow themselves to feel and learn with their hearts instead of over analyzing using their mental abilities, these extraordinary experiences will be much more frequent and a lot of fun. Horses have a lot to teach us and they can only do so when we are on a higher level on consciousness.

It has become common practice over the centuries to control our horses through domination. By creating pain/fear/discomfort to our horses in order to achieve our goals, we are asking them to be submissive and it is so common that we now call it "tradition". Shame on us! A horse's body translates exactly what is going on in his mind. If we are a source of pain and/or fear for our horses, we are speaking to their minds and giving them no reason to trust us or be friends with us. This is very obvious when working with a horse that has been abused, either on a physical or emotional level. Even if they feel our vibration to be kind and full of good will, it is very difficult for them to trust easily and let us handle them without putting up a fuss. The trainer has to be very patient and wait for the horse to be ready to accept more human contact if he is to get anywhere. No one can force an abused horse to trust a human. This can only happen if the human earns the horse's trust, respect and love. This can take only a few days or weeks. It can also take years, depending on the level of abuse and the horse's personality. There are some horses that never come around and are labelled "unsafe" to ride or handle. Ultimately, the choice is theirs to make. If these horses in need of rehabilitation never come across a human that they can trust entirely, they may choose to not ever cooperate with the specie again. Always keep in mind that horses communicate on a higher level of consciousness and they know what a human is thinking, what their ulterior motives are and, most importantly, what humans are capable of. Horses are prey animals, which means they never, ever forget experiences that put their safety and lives in jeopardy. Whenever pain, fear or discomfort is used to control a horse, the experience will be present in the equines mind for the rest of their lives. These experiences don't need to be extreme. Using a harsh bit when riding, or even a simple snaffle, is enough to create an experience that will forever stay in a horse's mind. Many will argue that their horses love the bit because they accept it with no problem. This is a human's interpretation, not the horses! Even if the horse accepts the bit politely when bridled, there can be many factors that explain this, for example, a nose-squeeze if they don't open up or a thumb stuck in their mouths, wiggling and pushing against their tender bars and tongue to force their mouth open. So, it's a lot easier to open up now and deal with the bit later. Keep in mind that horses are very submissive when it comes to pain and fear. When riding, if the horse doesn't "give to the bit", the pressure goes up and the pain increases. Do you honestly think that horses are enjoying this? Why is it that some equestrians can ride horses with absolutely no bit at all and have total control over them? Every equestrian discipline can be practiced safely with a bitless bridle. The difference lies in the rider, not the horse. Many bitted run away horses have been rehabilitated into happy bitless horses that are safe to ride just by dropping our dominant behaviour and methods of creating submissiveness.

Rehabilitating a horse with behaviour issues is no easy task. The process is easily compared to a human, child or adult, trying to deal and heal from abuse or violence in their lives. In such a case both horse and human need to find and believe in their true self again. This is usually done through careful guidance with an experienced professional, willing to listen and encourage the "patient/client" on their journey to healing. I'm not suggesting that only professional horse trainers should rehabilitate horses. Actually many non-professional horse handlers are better at rehabilitating horses simply because they are loving and patient and they do it for themselves, not as a business that needs to pull in profits. Also, time is not an issue so they allow the horse to progress at its own speed. This creates a very strong bond based on trust, respect and love which is the perfect combination for success, whether working with abused horses, children or adults.

We do not need to rack our brains on how to please our horses so that they won't buck us off. Instead, we need to look at what they really need from us rather than what we are willing to offer. Nobody likes to be in a relationship where they feel they have to do things a certain way so as to not upset their partner. Anytime you are holding back on what you really want to say or do you are not honouring who you really are, your true self. This is also a form of disrespect towards yourself. If you cannot respect yourself, how can you expect anybody else to respect you? This is often what happens to children at school. Bullying is a huge issue and whether the child is being bullied or is the bully, the underlying truth is that neither one of these children have self-respect. As we grow older, the same situations happen in the office or in a relationship instead of in the school yard, but it is no different. Whenever we feel that we are acting or saying words to please the other party, we are allowing them to manipulate and "bully" us. We are not respecting ourselves, our beliefs and values. Being authentic is empowering, even if the only person satisfied at the time is ourselves. In the long run, being authentic paves the way for a life full of richness because we end up attracting what we desire and believe in.

Horses are no different when it comes to authenticity. Within their own society, which we call a herd, if they allow another horse to push them around, they are basically telling them it's okay to be the leader. Mind you, there's nothing wrong with that among equines. Only certain types of personalities want to take on the role of leader in a horse herd because it comes with huge responsibilities. The leader has to find food, shelter and water for the herd as well as keep them safe at all times by being on guard. Horses don't kid around when it comes to hierarchy because the higher ranking horse is the one that can save your life. Horses do not know how to be anything else but authentic. They do not hide their emotions or pretend to like something when they actually don't. This makes them a little naive in the sense that they expect every interaction they have to be understood and based on authenticity, which includes interactions with humans.

Horses have been using emotion as a non-verbal language all along. These emotions are communicated through vibrational energy and telepathy. Some people may want to believe that this communication is not really taking place and it is only horses responding to body language. If this was true, it wouldn't be a very effective way of surviving and avoiding life threatening situations. What if horses were too far away from each other or trees obstructed their view to see the very subtle body language signals sent out by their leader? Their life would be in danger for not spotting that vital source of information. Also, horse's eyesight has been known to fail. It doesn't make any sense that horses would rely entirely on body language to communicate amongst each other.

As evidenced by increased heart rate and perspiration, emotions give off high frequencies and vibrations. Most species, except humans, use their senses to detect these vibrations and gather a lot of information in doing so (i.e. dogs smell fear). Humans have a hard time controlling their emotions and because horses "read" them so well, a human cannot hide their true emotions or feelings. They can't even pretend to hide their true feelings by expertly using the proper body language. Horses will always sense their vibration and know the underlying truth. That explains why horses are so good at equine-assisted therapy. A good human facilitator that has a close relationship with the equine co-facilitators used in this type of program will always know what the human client is really feeling.

Predator vs Prey vs Primate
When working with horses it is important to realize that quick and rapid movements are synonymous with predatorial behaviour. There are no slow moving predators in nature.

Although we talk a lot about humans being predators and horses as prey animals, we don't talk about the human as primate. We may be predators, meaning we eat meat, making us a threat to horses, but we are also primates which makes us an even harder animal to figure out in a horse's point of view.

Primates touch, feel, hold, pull and dominate with their hands. Observing monkeys shows you exactly how a primate (human) behaves. They quickly address another primate via their head, instead of setting boundaries and respecting this space like horses. Horses rarely have direct contact via the head. Stallions fighting for leadership are one example of head to head contact. We are comfortable with clutching, holding and petting like primates because it is innate to our specie but this behaviour is completely unnatural to horses. I witnessed a human owner holding a new born foal by its neck and hind-quarters like it was a toy with complete disregard for the panic this foal was expressing. The owner seemed to have no idea the effect her actions had on the foal and even naively mentioned how important imprinting is. We as primates always meet a horse and go directly to the head disregarding the personal space of the horse. The horse may or may not want contact and it's only option is to leave. Can you imagine a dominant person walking up to you and while saying hello pats you on top of your head without being invited to even get that close to you? That action is typical of an adult with a child and demonstrates the superior status of the adult even if it is not intended. Primate (human) behaviour brings on a whole new set of body language, vibrational energy and communication to the horse/human relationship. This is confusing to horses and gives them a lot to think about. We need to be aware that not only are we predators, but that as primates we are grabbers which is a foreign concept for horses.

NATURAL HORSE TRAINING

4

"Too many natural horsemanship techniques offer quick, easy fixes to problems without looking at the entire situation. If you're not looking at the whole picture, you're not seeing the whole picture."

- B-A King

Photo courtesy Hoof Print Publishing

One of the most controversial questions and statements I hear is "Why talk about natural horsemanship when it isn't even natural to ride a horse in the first place. The structure of their backs and bodies are not meant to carry a human."

For many years now I have been challenging this statement. Contrary to popular belief, I believe it is natural to ride a horse, but not based on our terms and conditions. The horse's back offers a solid and comfortable place to sit, right over their centre of gravity. If ridden properly, a horse will understand everything we are communicating to them simply by sitting balanced, our centre of gravity over theirs. In the Relationship Riding philosophy, if a horse does not want us to ride them, they simply let us know by not letting us get on. They have a voice and are allowed to use it. They are not punished or reprimanded if they do not allow us to get on, quite the contrary. If this happens, we need to listen to the horse's reasons for not allowing a rider up on their back. There can be a million different reasons why the horse does not allow this and the rider might never know what the real reason is. So be it! I personally will not climb on the back of a 1000lb animal that doesn't want me up there. I will also not force my way on him by threatening him with "unpleasantness" (a nicer word for "abuse"). Here are some of the reasons we might "hear" our horses telling us when they do not allow us to climb on their backs:

"Who are you?": If you haven't seen your horse in over a week or so (each horse is different and some will enjoy independence more than others so the time factor is irrelevant here) and decide to just walk over, halter them and go for a ride, the horse has every right to say "Whoa buddy! How do I know that you're safe to be around? I am very comfortable and safe being in my horse herd right now. I see no logical reason to leave my herd. You haven't proven yourself a good leader to me yet."

Every single day horses check up on their leader to see if she/he is still the protective one that they can count on. Why would it be any different with a human? This situation also explains why some horses become very buddy or barn sour. They simply don't believe that they will be safe with us. If we lose it and start yanking the shank and applying pressure on them, we only make the matter worse and then they truly have every right to not believe in our leadership skills.

The saddle doesn't fit: As an equine sports massage therapist I have learned and experienced first-hand how much damage an ill-fitting saddle can cause a horse. The fact that horses are extremely tolerant and will endure a lot of pain before actually "saying" anything about it doesn't make it easier for us to detect a saddle fitting problem. Just to give you a heads up on how serious a problem this is, over 80% of the clients I visit ride their horses with saddles that don't fit. The remaining 20% use saddles that are just okay, not necessarily comfortable for the horse. Here's a funny fact: every one of these riders with ill-fitting saddles fully enjoy the saddles for themselves and find them to be very comfortable, especially the ones that were custom made and cost a huge amount of money! So, tell me, who's riding whom? A horse should not have to accept any situation that causes them pain and discomfort simply because we decided it was okay and more comfortable for us.

Mounting and dismounting: Whenever we are holding on to the horn or pommel to heave ourselves up into the saddle, we are creating huge discomfort on the horse's spine. After a while, the horse's only way of letting us know that this is uncomfortable is to move around when we are trying to get on or off. There are ways to mount and dismount a horse, without pulling their spines out of alignment, that is comfortable for both horse and rider (yes, this also applies to those of you who ride in treeless saddles and I am one of them.)

"My back is sore": We all have our off days and our horses are no different. If you are riding a school horse, you might have a horse that

deals with all of the above mentioned issues plus many, many more that I am running out of space to talk about and that are unknown to us humans. So, you may come across a horse that is simply off, sore, tight and the idea of carrying a rider is simply not appealing to them, especially if this rider is a student that lacks balance, finesse with their hands and patience. This state of mind can be difficult to understand since pinpointing the exact problem can be very difficult. Humans seem to need a reason for everything and sometimes things just are because they are. It's that simple. Maybe the previous rider kicked the air out of this horse for a whole hour and its bruised ribs can't take much more. If you are the only rider for a particular horse and you have eliminated the above scenarios, your horse could simply have a sore back or a pulled muscle from kicking around outside with his/her buddies. This is more frequent in the Spring when the ground is slippery and wet with mud. If your horse is lucky enough to be living in a natural environment, sharing its pasture with the same species, they could have been in the middle of dealing with a situation when you walked up and took them away. Another common scenario is the box-stalled horse that only has approximately 10' x 10' to move around in (no running, stretching, or laying down comfortably in a clean spot, and nothing else to do except stare at metal bars). Did you know that for a human to keep healthy it is recommended that they walk 10,000 steps every day? A box-stalled horse will on average take only 800 steps, this for an animal that should be walking 15 – 30 miles per day. Can you imagine the emotional distress this causes? When the owner decides they are going out for a ride for one hour of intensive exercise, that horse might not be too cooperative, with reason. Whatever the situation, your horse is trying to let you know that being ridden today is not on their mind, only on yours.

So, can a horse let us know, without a doubt, that they are okay with you getting on? There is one way to know for sure and that is to experiment, which is what I did with one of my Azteca mares, Angelica. Although Angelica had the traditional 30-day training on her, she hadn't been ridden in 1 ½ years when I purchased her. She has never been ridden in a traditional manner (except for those 30 days) and I never used a bit, a treed saddle or shoes on her. She lives in a natural environment outside, interacting naturally with her own specie in a mixed herd, wandering around all day looking for food. Angelica has always been allowed to express herself and give her opinion on what I'm doing. She knows I will listen attentively to her and our mutual respect for one another makes for a very authentic relationship. One day I decided to see if she really was okay with me riding her or was she just responding to me because she knew what I was asking of her. I stood on the mounting block in a small indoor arena. Angelica had no halter, lead rope or any kind of tack on her. I made sure my body was very quiet and I did not speak a word or make any kind of sound to influence her. I just stood on the block, breathing deeply in order to connect with her. She walked up to me and put her nose on my heart chakra, in the middle of my chest. I communicated with her using telepathy and vibrational energy, as described in the previous chapter. I told her that if she wanted me to get on her back and ride she would come and pick me up by placing herself in a position where I was able to get on. With her first steps she walked away from me, but only far enough to turn around and face me, parallel to the mounting block, but not close enough for me to get on. Again, I stayed still with no words, gestures or sounds. I communicated my thoughts again, making sure she knew that I was only going to get on if she wanted me to. She then took a few more steps towards me but still not enough for me to get on her back. I could have easily touched her nose or done something to encourage her to take just one more step, but instead I stayed true to my word and just waited. At that moment, she walked up to the mounting block, stopped at exactly the right spot and stuck her belly out, offering her back to me. I gently pet her, thanking her for her trust, and slipped onto her back. We rode for a little bit, without me giving her any direction. She took me around the arena a few times, doing figure 8's, sometimes stopping for a brief moment at the gate. When she was done taking me on a tour, she stopped and I immediately knew it was time to get off because she was not going to move anymore. I slipped off and we shared a big hug (horses do hug each other by putting their head over another horse's neck and pulling them in). This experience proved to me without any doubt that horses are willing to communicate with us and do so on a regular basis.

We don't notice it because we aren't paying attention and they are not speaking English (or French, or Spanish, etc.). But if we open up our channels of communication, we will quickly realize that they are talking to us all the time. They also have no problem with us riding them as long as we are respectful instead of being demanding and dominant. It is so easy to throw a horse off balance simply by wiggling in the saddle, sitting back, leaning forward or tightening up because we are nervous or exasperated with our mount. If we allow them to move in a balanced way, it becomes easier for them to carry us and the whole riding experience becomes a fun one for both horse and rider. My mare has always been ridden this way so when I asked her to come and pick me up, she knew that it would be a comfortable and fun experience for her and that she wouldn't have to deal with a difficult rider. That's why she offered me her back and took me for a ride. I have also heard of people experiencing this with wild horses; more proof that it is natural to ride a horse.

Natural Horsemanship

All riding/training methods have in common a constant: to impose your will on a horse using force. The horse, being a prey animal, interprets all repressive action as a predatorial act. This is where all misunderstanding between horse and human originates. (B. Gentili, 1997)

The expression "natural horsemanship" is not only overused these days, it's also misused. Natural horsemanship shows us how to teach a horse to move away from pressure, gently and with no resistance. In order to do this we must create pain and/or discomfort to the horse by applying progressive pressure until they move away. This explains why some riders wear spurs. A horse's natural survival instincts tells him to do the opposite; move into pressure in the hope of killing, or at least getting rid of, the predator hanging onto its neck or belly. Have you ever watched the wild animal show on television where an innocent antelope gets attacked by a hungry predator (they usually show a large cat to make the scene more interesting)? Notice how the antelope goes right down in the hope of crushing or getting rid of the predator. It might not actually seem as if he is doing that when we watch it, but it is a tactic these prey animals use in order to survive. They push into pressure, not away from it, because this could cause a lot of damage if something with huge claws was hanging onto their neck.

So what is the difference between natural horsemanship and riding/training a horse naturally, the Relationship Riding way?

When horses determine their position in a herd, they do so by pushing each other around. They point their noses towards each other's flanks to push them forward. They also put pressure on the opponent's barrel to turn the horse towards them. No one pulls or bonks heads, there's no unbalanced weight on their backs and there is no leather tack to hinder the horse's natural movement and liberty. As horses push each other around like that, hierarchy is established amongst them, as well as trust and respect. When a human being manages to communicate in this manner with horses, he establishes himself as a potential leader for the whole herd or for his two-horse herd; himself and his horse. I say "potential" because he still hasn't proven himself to be a consistent and truthful leader in the eyes of the horse. The human still has to earn the trust and respect from the other member of his personal herd: his horse. If it takes a while to accomplish this, humans will often think this technique doesn't really work and that there is an easier way to do it. That's when human ego kicks in and the fragile relationship that was slowly developing between horse and human is now in jeopardy. Humans impose their will on their horses, demanding and controlling their every move and thought. Because no physical pain is seemingly being done to the horse then it's considered okay. For some reason many humans don't think that it's important to pay attention to a horse's intellectual and emotional mind set. Anthropomorphism, attributing human personality traits to an animal, is also worth mentioning. Humans make up excuses for their horses and when these excuses label horses with human traits, it sets the scene for misinterpretation of what is really going on. Horses have their own emotional systems and they do not react to the same things nor do they react the same way as we do to situations. I often observe people working with their horses and acting/talking to them as if their horse was human, imposing their own expectations on their animal. If they are not getting the expected results from their horses, then the horses are labelled with a variety of character traits (i.e. stupid, stubborn, lazy, etc) simply because the humans are unable to explain why the horse is reacting the way he is. This is explained by the fact that humans do not understand why their horses are reacting/acting the way they are so the easiest solution is to interpret the horse's reaction based on human behaviour, i.e. typically how the human would have reacted if they were dealing with a similar situation. A human's interpretation of horse behaviour can also be an indicator of that person's own personal life-management skills. For example, I was trying to saddle a horse with a treeless saddle for the owner to try out. The horse moved around constantly, trying to get rid of his owner. He did not see her as a leader so pushing her around was the natural thing to do so that he could go back to his feed bowl. After a little while, I politely offered my help and the owner handed over the lead rope. I walked away with that horse and in less than three minutes I walked back with an entirely different horse. He was respecting my space and standing still for me without being tied up. I even walked up to his feed bowl, stopped and then walked away without him putting up a fight. All he needed to know was who the leader was. But, the owner saw nothing of this and even when it was explained to her, she believed nothing of what I said. Instead, she chose to believe that her horse missed his pasture buddy, was hungry, didn't like the wind, was nervous because of the tractor in the distance (although he showed no sign of nervousness at all), etc. The excuses went on and on. I could only do so much, this owner just was not seeing what the horse was trying to tell her. It is a form of denial and admitting to a lack of knowledge is not necessarily easy, no matter how diplomatic and kind the people around you are being. My concern in a case like this is always the owner's safety, but there wasn't a lot more I could do after offering lessons, clinics, etc. This horse owner wasn't ready to see things differently. Luckily, she has a very kind and loving horse and I honestly think he would not deliberately harm her.

There are a number of horse training techniques available to the public. It can become very confusing (for both horse and owner!) to make any sense of all of this. Some of these techniques are controversial, others are either very complicated or easy, and some make absolutely no sense at all. These techniques cater to different horse disciplines too, which adds another element of confusion.

It does not have to be complicated because it all actually boils down to only two techniques. In every horse training technique available to the public, whether it is traditional, classical training, western or natural horsemanship, there are basically only two ways of training a horse, *any* horse: 1. The dominant/controlling method and 2. The non-dominant/non-controlling method.

1. The dominant/controlling way, using pain, fear or discomfort to force the horse to accept what we want, better known as negative reinforcement.

2. In the non-dominant/non-controlling way, horses willingly do for us what we want because they don't worry about pain, discomfort or fear and they can move away from the situation whenever it gets too confusing and scary (work at liberty). This is referred to as positive reinforcement.

At some point both techniques get the results and the job done. The difference is in how long the results last and what was damaged along the way. Let's take a look at these two methods in more detail.

1. Dominant/controlling approach
Results through pain, fear and discomfort often get horses responding rapidly because they "give in", or become submissive. Horses learn rapidly to avoid pain, even if we are making the "wrong answer uncomfortable and the right answer easy". This is commonly used in today's natural horsemanship techniques as well as classical training around the world. These training techniques use negative responses in the horse to get the point across. These methods do not build strong relationships between horse and rider because there is always a lack of trust and respect between the two. Many of you will challenge this statement saying that you have a wonderful relationship with your horse and that he/she does everything you ask of them. To this I respond do not confuse a subservient horse as being one that enjoys a relationship with you. Would you respect anyone that gets what they want from you all the time without taking into consideration what you like or dislike, or what you can and can't do? How do you define bullying? Would you love them more and

want to hang out with them all the time? The horse's willingness to have a relationship with humans that use these methods isn't based on an equal status between man and animal but rather on a man's dominant relationship with a subservient animal.

After using these methods, in time, "issues" start showing up: horses become harder to catch and need to be bribed with food, horses won't let themselves be bridled or saddled without showing resistance, they are not as much fun to ride because they are herd bound, etc. Horses will also lack "ground manners" (i.e. push you around with their heads and bodies, frisk you for treats, and the list goes on). Although we may think they haven't learned to be polite, in horse language this behaviour simply means that you are lower in the hierarchy and they are a better leader than you, so they push you around and prove their leadership position as long as you accept it and allow it. Sometimes, none of these signs show up but there is a great sadness to be seen in the horse's eyes, which most humans do not see (this is usually when we hear humans say that they have a great relationship with their horse because he obeys perfectly). Do any of these situations with horses sound familiar to you? Unfortunately, when the horse's behaviour starts to change they are easily labelled as "stupid, stubborn, and sour" (I am being polite here!). No need to say that the results obtained through negative reinforcement are not durable and lasting. Somewhere down the road, the horse will find a way to let you know that they have had enough of your bullying and are not going to take it anymore. Lucky for us dominating humans, horses are extremely kind, gentle and very, very, tolerant as well as forgiving towards us. The level of subservience differs from one horse to the other.

2. Non-dominant/non-controlling approach

Results obtained through willingness forces the human to forget about his ego and controlling habits and engage in an authentic relationship, with himself as well as with the horse. Humans must learn to feel and be aware of their own surroundings by waking up all their senses. They must enter the horse's world and understand it from the horse's point of view. Humans must also learn how a horse thinks and I'm not talking about making up excuses or explanations to why their horses act the way they do, but really learning why they are getting a certain type of behaviour from their horse. Only then will they be able to understand the knowledge horses are willing to pass on to us resulting in authentic partners in this new relationship. When horses know that there is no pain, discomfort or fear coming their way and they have a good leader, they are willing to play with us and discover things together. They don't mind us getting on their backs and will often offer their back for us to climb on. When you are in a relationship based on love, respect, trust, harmony and authenticity, whether it be human/human or human/animal, discovering life and new adventures together is fun and exciting, not threatening and scary. Even trying something out for the first time would be okay if you were allowed to walk away as soon as it becomes scary, uncomfortable or painful.

Natural Horsemanship vs Relationship Riding

Some of you may be wondering what the difference is between the so-called natural horsemanship techniques that are very popular and the Relationship Riding method. Allow me to clarify.

Relationship Riding is based on a philosophy, not a recipe. This philosophy allows the horse to have a voice and an opinion. It is not a philosophy where humankind imposes its agenda on an animal, but rather it seeks to see what the animal has to teach humankind and how beneficial it can be to both parties. This technique is natural to the horse, which means we do not need to teach it to move away from pressure by poking him. Instead our bodies communicate very clearly to the horse what we want, on the ground as well as in the saddle. If the horse accepts our leadership then there is no resistance and he/she responds to us smoothly and happily. It is no different than dancing with someone. When two people are good dance partners, they will move across the dance floor effortlessly and they don't need to push their partner around in order to do so. Their bodies communicate silently, moving in perfect symbiosis, stopping and going, turning and twisting, and fully enjoying the whole process.

Horses are not meant to be dominated: nature is rife with species dominating others, such as killer bees and humans. A fear-based response to our demands resembles a dictatorship, not the type of leadership that earns you respect and trust. Although natural horsemanship does not come across as being a fear-based technique, it is asking the horse to execute a task properly. If the horse fails to do so, the pressure is increased until the task is executed as demanded. This pressure causes fear, confusion and discomfort in the horse and can sometimes lead to pain (depending on the trainer's level of tolerance that day.) I have personally witnessed how far the level of pressure can be increased and emphatically reject this abuse. These acts of violence were performed by well-known trainers that justified their actions to the crowd, saying the horse was extremely disobedient, resistant and deserved the treatment. Keep in mind that signals can be ambiguous to horses. Dominating a horse is easy and we have been told to do it for many centuries. That is probably why we do it so much and believe it is the only way to go about controlling such a big, strong animal. It is also how we justify our violent behaviour. No one will ever attain an authentic, close, loving, resistance-free relationship by dominating a horse. All these popular natural horsemanship techniques that are well-known today use negative reinforcement (make the wrong answer difficult and the right answer easy). In this type of training the horses don't get a chance to say "no" without having to pay the consequences. Their voices are silenced. This is no different than being in an abusive relationship or bullying situation where you have to obey or else you will have painful consequences, where you have no chance of expressing yourself or initiating anything on your own. It is not uncommon during a natural horsemanship clinic to see the facilitator trying to "fix" the horses by teaching them how to give to pressure, walk off on a certain foot, turn properly, etc. It isn't often that bad saddle fitting is taken into consideration either. Do not kid yourself: our horses always respond to us based on what we are asking, how we are feeling and the level of respect we are putting into this relationship. Also, you must believe that horses already know how to walk, turn and they know better than us what is the most appropriate foot to use in order to keep their balance, at all times. No matter how many different programs, clinics and levels of natural horsemanship you do, if you are being a dictator you will not have a truly happy horse, no matter how obedient he is. One day, you might find yourself in a compromising situation. For example, you might fall off your horse and have your foot hung up in the stirrup or hands caught up in the reins. Your horse will then have a choice to take off because you are no longer "in charge" or he'll stop and give you a chance to get back on, like a true partner. If you are hoping for a true partnership, start giving back what you would like to receive and treat your partner accordingly. If you think this is a little farfetched, think again. It has happened to me more than once. A horse I was riding one day spooked quite unexpectedly and violently. The explosive energy that comes from a horse that is much heavier and stronger than you will cause your centre of gravity to shift and you will lose your balance. No matter how experienced a rider you are, it happens to every one of us. In this case, I lost my seat and was launched forward, to the right of my horse. The next thing I knew this horse stopped dead in her tracks and held me up with her neck in a weird, unnatural position. Horses know when you lose your balance and can't stay on their backs. That's why they are so good at bucking us off when they decide they have had enough. This mare didn't want me off but instead wanted to help me find my balanced position again to prevent me from crashing to the ground. Another similar story happened when I was rehabilitating an abused horse. I was riding him calmly in a small open field when he decided he had gone as far away as he could handle from the field gate. So instead of walking back calmly to the gate, he picked up a trot that turned into a canter, which evolved into a full blown gallop. This horse is a very big and powerful Morgan and there was no stopping him until he had reached that gate. So, I rode the gallop (which was actually very smooth and agreeable!), praying that he wouldn't buck me off or jump the fence (he is known for jumping out of 5' round pens!). Once we arrived at the gate, he stood quietly while I dismounted, landing on shaky legs! I realized that this horse had no intention of getting rid of me because it would have been very easy for him to buck me off. He just needed to get back to his safe spot, in this case it was at the gate where we entered the field. If I hadn't gone out so far, he would probably just have walked faster or trotted back to his safe spot instead of cantering. The fact that I remained cooperative with him, willing to listen to his concerns and allowed him to express himself, kept the trust between us strong. He didn't feel threatened by me and received no pain, fear or discomfort for doing something he believed was necessary. After dismounting, he started walking away backwards, afraid of retribution. I walked over to him with a loving heart, petting him and thanking him for keeping me safe. He then followed me around like a puppy without me holding his reins or leading him, no longer needing to be in his safe spot by the gate. Over all, this experience helped him gain confidence and deepened our relationship to a level that could never be acquired using traditional methods or negative reinforcement. Other trainers would say that this horse will always run away since he has gotten away with it and has been "taught" to do so. I beg to differ. There is a reason why this beautiful black horse ended up in the feed lot and I believe it has more to do with him being misunderstood and punished for bad behaviour for 12 years. In using the Relationship Riding approach with him, I have discovered a very gentle and loving soul in this massive and powerful horse. I have helped him deal with his insecurities, slowly, one at a time, on his own accord, and he has become a very close friend to me. He even stands guard beside me, as if to protect me, when strangers enter the field.

Please keep in mind that no matter how much we love our horses and want them to be happy and healthy, most of them come to us with a history that isn't always pretty. In their point of view, we are predators with the ability to cause a lot of pain and fear. Horses will not forget their past memories, even if they live in the moment, and as genuine leaders and horse owners, it is our job to help them overcome situations and the behaviours they have developed. Whether we understand or not what is going on in their minds, harsh punishment and imposing our agenda on them without their consent is not a way to be a true friend. Thus, we should not expect true friendship in return.

Many elements will make a situation different for a horse and a human. For example, either partner may be having a bad day and giving off unpleasant vibrations. These elements must be taken into consideration every time we interact with a horse. Their sense of flight is a survival instinct that has been instilled in them for thousands of years. This instinct will always take over when a horse is scared to death in any given situation, as described in my earlier example of the runaway Morgan. But if you have a strong relationship, your scared horse will turn to you for leadership and guidance and will calm right down when they realize and believe you are calm and will keep them safe.

A horse's reaction to various stimuli is very unpredictable. Because horses are as individual as we are, there is no sure way of knowing what they are going to do next. The best we can do is to try and understand them, listen to what they have to say, and not get offended when they are not doing what we ask them to. In other words, try to be the best friend your horse ever had. The effort is worth it and he will give it back tenfold.

Relationship Riding is not a recipe. There are no recipes when it comes to having a relationship with a horse, no more than a recipe for a great relationship with a spouse or a child. Each individual must adapt to the other and put in as much unconditional love as they wish to receive.

The trust and bond that we establish in a relationship with our horses is not transferrable. In other words, you cannot train horses to act the same with everyone as they act with the person that they have developed a bond and relationship with. It is each rider's responsibility to make sure they have a good relationship with the horse they are about to mount. If you think about it, it is no different than human beings. A child does not have the same relationship with their mother as they have with their father. The level of trust and honesty will vary based on the bond they develop. That being said, horses all respond to a good leader in the same way. It doesn't take very long for a horse to recognize the leadership in us, and it makes for a much safer and happier experience with our equine friends.

5

"In the steady gaze of the horse shines a silent eloquence that speaks of love and loyalty, strength and courage. It is the window that reveals to us how willing is his spirit, how generous his heart."

- Author Unknown

Photo courtesy Hoof Print Publishing

One of the things you need to keep in mind with the Relationship Riding technique is that your emotions and intent are a huge part of the equation. Your physical body might execute moves perfectly but if it contradicts with the way you are feeling or thinking, the latter will take over and you will not get the desired results. As human beings we have the tendency to do things perfectly with our physical bodies but we totally ignore what feelings or intentions we are putting into these physical efforts, creating ambiguity. Horses pick up very quickly on what our intentions really are, simply because as prey animals they are in tune with the vibrations that emanate from predators like humans. This is how they survive in the wild, as well as in some domestic situations. In order to achieve harmony while riding, we need to put more awareness on our inner self and on what the horse is communicating to us rather than on the technique itself.

One of the first things you must do is prepare yourself to give up your dominant role and become more passive. You must allow your body to follow the movement of the horse. The "Ultimate Union with Your Horse" can only be achieved when the rider absorbs the movement offered by the horse with his/her own body. It is important that the rider doesn't interfere with the horse's natural movement and balance. In order to do this, the rider must be aware of how his body can ultimately unbalance a horse. One analogy that works well here is to imagine that a person is sitting on your shoulders. Every small movement they make, whether it is leaning forward, sideways or backwards, you will feel it tenfold and it will probably throw you off balance, even with a small child on your back. In order for you to move forward easily, the rider on your shoulders will not only have to sit quietly but he will also have to make a great effort to maintain his own balance and move with you. Now imagine that this person starts getting worried, angry or impatient and that you have no clue what is causing this reaction in them. Your "rider's" body will tighten up and become very stiff. He will then start pushing you in different directions and maybe even raise his voice when you are not getting it. Wouldn't you want to just throw this person off your shoulders, which are probably stiff and sore by now? How in the world are you supposed to know what the rider wants when, first of all, all the tightness in his/her body makes it impossible for you to understand the message? The line of communication is broken and they become more and more demanding on you. This is what your horse goes through every time he/she is ridden by a rider that focuses strictly on performance without taking into consideration who is carrying them.

We must keep in mind that a horse's balance is fragile and easily disturbed. It is not the horse's responsibility to make riding easy for us. Remember, we are the ones that decided to ride them in the first place! It becomes our responsibility to ride quietly, relaxed and to allow the horse to move our bodies in synchronicity with theirs without disturbing their natural balance. In other words, the rider must allow his lower body to move freely, without any resistance, as the horse's back gently moves the rider. When riding a horse, the rider must keep his upper body still and well balanced over the horse's centre of gravity and not use reins for balance. Equal weight is put on each seat bone and it is connected to each side of the horse's spine. Imagine your seat bones as an electrical plug in a wall socket. If the plug is pulled out to one side, you won't get a full connection and the appliance you plugged in won't work properly. It is no different when it comes to the rider's seat bones and the horse's back. If the rider wants the horse to know where to go and at what speed, it is a must for that rider to have his seat bones connected to the horse to communicate this. When two bodies are moving in synchronicity, there needs to be a reliable connection, like in dancing. When one dancer stops moving the other one automatically knows it is time to stop. There is no need to physically hurt the other dancer by using a metal tool (i.e. a bit) in order to communicate this to them. If the dancing partner hesitates to stop, then they are disconnected and the message is not coming across clearly. In dancing, this means the dancer's "frame" is too weak and they have lost their point of contact. This explains why communication doesn't work once the rider starts building tension. In most cases the first area to tighten up when we are riding is the seat muscles and hands. When we tighten our seat we are disconnecting the seat bones from the horse's spine by putting muscles and flesh between the spine and our bones, a little like a big pillow. We also become less balanced and start making it harder for the horse to advance in a balanced manner. With tension our centre of gravity rises into our chest and we become unstable, also known as being "top heavy". Our hands tighten up and create unnecessary pain and discomfort on the horse's mouth as well as conflicting signals.

The rider's pelvis must be slightly tilted forward in a "neutral" position that allows it to move freely back and forth. Try sitting on a big exercise ball and rocking your pelvis back and forth. If your pelvis is "locked" in place (i.e. tilted backwards) you will be unable to move the ball comfortably. This resistance will immediately create a lack of communication between horse and rider as the horse's back tries to move with the rider and is greeted by a locked pelvis. The neutral pelvis will greet the motion of the horse's back and move with it, not against it. Nothing should be forced that would create tightness and resistance. This position should feel natural and comfortable. With the pelvis in a neutral position, seat bones connected and tailbone down, the rider's belly should feel soft and ready to absorb the movement coming from the horse's back (this is not a time to tuck in your tummy in order to look good!). The rider's pelvis and tummy acts as a "buffer" for the horse's movements and it must be passive and free of any tension in order to offer a continuous connection with the horse's back. All of the horse's motions are absorbed and equalized from below the rider's navel.

The rider's legs must lie quietly on the sides of the horse. Any pressure from one or both legs can or will be interpreted by the horse as a signal to do something or go somewhere. It is no different from having a buddy ride on our shoulders. When they start tightening their leg muscles or poking us, we will think they are trying to tell us something so we will turn left or right in the hope of doing what they are asking.

The upper body also plays an important role in riding horses. It must be very still and not lean backward, forward or sideways. This would be interpreted by the horse as a change in direction or change in gait. Always try to imagine what it would feel like if you had a person sitting on your shoulders doing the same things we do as a rider to our horses. It can become quite confusing for horses to figure out what our bodies are telling them. It is imperative that each rider realize how important every movement of their body affects the horse. We haven't even talked about reins or hands yet and already we have what it takes to throw our horses completely off balance. Now imagine for a moment that you are also very upset about work or family matters or the way your horse is progressing. Tension is building up in your body, your centre of gravity is moving from below your belt to your upper body creating an imbalance and your line of communication in your seat is disconnected causing your horse to not know what you want. In other words, you are not physically and emotionally in harmony with your horse. We must give our horses credit for being so tolerant with us!

Our horses need their heads when they are moving in order to keep their bodies in perfect balance. You may have noticed that when a horse walks around, his head bobs over the front leg that is touching the ground. The momentum of movement that goes up their hind leg and through their backs in a waving motion follows through to their heads and is then returned downward through their front leg. This is the way a horse moves naturally. When we tie up their heads or restrain its movement with reins, we are preventing the horse from moving freely and smoothly, in a balanced and natural way. In order to connect the energy that flows freely from our horses' backs and through our pelvis to their heads, we need to use our hands. Hold the reins just short enough to feel the weight of your horse's head. Your hands should lie in front of you, as if you are holding a small book, not resting on a pommel or horn, and be ready and willing to move as soon as the horse does. To allow the horse to take the first step forward, your hands should be slightly forward (keep in mind that the horse needs his head to move) and ready to move back to their original position as the horse's head comes back. In other words, you will be bringing your hands/elbows back to your hips and allow them to go forward again when the horse requests your hands forward through the natural movement of his head. I call this the "hip to hand connection" and I see immediate changes in a horse that is ridden this way simply because my body is moving in harmony with his and his natural balance is not disturbed. You don't even have to worry about timing it properly. When your hips go forward, your hands will naturally come back towards them. As long as your hips and shoulders are relaxed, this movement will happen naturally. Try it on the ground first. Bend your knees, pretending to be sitting on a horse, and move your pelvis like a horse would. Hold a pair of invisible reins and allow your shoulders/elbows/arms to be relaxed. Watch how your hands come back towards your hips as they move forward. You can also try this on a fitness ball. When you ride a horse with this hip-to-hand connection, the horse's ears will turn towards you in full attention while his head stays very still between your hands, waiting to see what will be requested of him next. You will have your horse's focus and attention. If you start tugging or pulling on the reins because the horse is not responding like you would like him to, you will ruin any little bit of trust and respect you have established and will have to work very hard at getting it back. As mentioned previously respect goes a long way and when the rider isn't pulling, tugging or balancing on the reins, they are telling the horse they respect their space, i.e. their heads. Whether you choose to use a bit or not is up to you. Personally, I haven't used a bit in a horse's mouth since I developed this technique back in the mid 1990's. No matter what the horse's issues are (i.e. running through the bit, high-headed, over-flexed during collection, etc.) if I ride them in a way that is natural to them and comprehensible, they will gladly stay with me with no intention of running away or bucking me off. This happens because I am being respectful and we are having a conversation with our bodies where the horse has a voice.

We cannot expect horses to be ridden in collection unless they are happy, balanced and understanding what the rider wants. I am talking about natural collection here, not a movement that is forced out of the horse by using harsh bits and various equipment that causes pain, discomfort or fear. When natural collection occurs, the horse is moving freely and willingly, creating a movement of great beauty while the rider's body is in perfect harmony with the horse. It is difficult to miss. This can be accomplished when the rider allows the horse to teach them how to ride. Horses have known all along how to self-collect, do flying lead changes and to pick up a canter on the right lead. Throughout the years, human beings have "taught" these movements to horses when they were ridden, instead of collaborating with horses and learning how to ask and ride these movements already well-known to horses.

Our goal when riding horses should be to move in perfect synchronicity with them, allowing them to show us their world, carrying us into a physical and spiritual experience, allowing us to enjoy the "Ultimate union with a horse".

The nature of human beings dictates that we rule with force, thus using our hands. The nature of the horse rules with harmony, trust, respect and love. If we wish to accomplish anything with horses, we must let go, literally, and start communicating more effectively in a language that is natural and clear to the horse.

Most of the time, we don't realize that we are the ones creating the miscommunication between horse and rider. We only think our horse is misbehaving and not getting it. We wonder why our riding session started out so well but now all hell has let loose.

A HORSE'S DEFINITION OF ...

6

"The wagon rests in winter, the sleigh in summer, the horse never."

-Yiddish proverb

Photo courtesy Hoof Print Publishing

There are many ways a horse tries to communicate with us and there are also many areas where we need to improve our communication in order to be understood.

One thing we need to change is our mind set and the way we think. Too often, we interpret certain reactions from our horses incorrectly. I believe the main reason we do this is because we are not allowing our minds to be flexible to see what is truly going on. There is also peer pressure and ego that come into play as well as hundreds of years of tradition. We turned off our intuition a long time ago and even if it keeps talking to us on a daily basis, we refuse to listen to it.

Listed below are some very important qualities that every horse person should possess in order to achieve success with horses. But these qualities are based on the horse's definitions and point of views, not ours. This information was channelled to me by my "teachers", horse ancestors and Spirit Horse.

How Horses Define

Consistency: persistence and consistency are two very important qualities but they are not rigid terms as we may think. Being consistent does not mean never changing your mind about something, especially when we are exposed to knowledge or information about a subject.

For many human beings, consistency plainly means "always doing the same thing the same way, no matter what". But consistency also means knowing what you want to do and doing so accordingly. I see many people trying to learn a certain method of training and if they don't get results quick enough, they are off to see another clinician to learn still another method, hoping that the "secret" will be revealed clearly this time and that effortlessly their horses will respond like magic. It is one thing to find out everything you can about certain methods of training and another to skim the surface and then quickly move on to the next horsemanship guru. I encourage everyone to learn as much as they can and research what is available out there. As a horse owner, it becomes your responsibility to use methods and techniques that resonate well with you and your horse. But, do take the time to fully understand the technique, not just the first level, before writing it off and moving on to something else.

I don't mean to disappoint anyone but there is no magic, although sometimes it feels like there is and it even looks like it. No matter what you choose to do, you will have to put effort and consistency into your relationship with your horse in order to get any kind of results.

In a horse's point of view, consistency means that your intentions towards him/her will always remain the same, whether the horses are being good or bad or whether they are quick to understand you or not on any given day. Consistency is similar to what we want from our relationship with our loved ones; unconditional love. To a horse, consistency means always doing what needs to be done "now" while still acting with respect, trust, authenticity and love. True consistency recognizes the inner voice or intuition and listens to it, without questioning or wavering. This means your intentions will always be consistent.

Clarity: I repeat this often to my students: Horses do not understand ambiguity. One of the main reasons why humans are not clear with horses is because we care first and foremost about what our plans are and we focus on them. We question ourselves, double check our agendas, go back and forth with different scenarios until we have our horses totally confused (especially if we follow a variety of training techniques but we don't adhere to one in particular). Humans need to recognize that the "external energy" they give off is directly connected to the "inner energy". They cannot pretend to want one thing when, deep inside, they are expecting another. Clarity comes with no ambiguous attachments and enables the horse to trust and respect the human being on a deeper level. Keep in mind that horses communicate through telepathy which gives them the ability to read our minds (whether we like it or not!). When our minds are racing from one idea to the next, our horses see this as being very confusing. By being in the moment and only having clear thoughts in our minds, our horses can relate to us better.

Flexibility: This is not an easy quality for humans to possess. In our society, we are very resistant to change, whether it is at home, at school or in the office. For many, being flexible means being weak (this is especially true for parents).

From the horse's point of view, flexibility is a quality that only smart beings possess. Flexibility is an important quality if you are a horse and need to adapt to the frequent changes in your life (i.e. weather, food, herd mates, owners, predators, etc.). A leader that can adapt quickly, easily and basically without flinching emotionally is flexible, thus trustworthy. You probably have heard horse people say "we've been doing things this way forever and it works, so why change?" Well here's a piece of information for the inflexible humans out there: horses are just as unpredictable, different, and have their own minds as we do. Some of the ways we have been training horses have given results for the wrong reasons because we did not take into consideration their character type and their personalities. We have been inflexible to changing these ways probably from fear of being negatively labelled by our peers. Also, we have better horse knowledge today, thus we have the information available to make appropriate changes. This is a big factor in the popularity of natural horsemanship. Harsh training methods were shunned and looked down upon. If we look back in history, we will also find that the reasons we were doing things a certain way no longer exist (i.e. we do not need horses to carry our equipment across battlefields, which is the reason why treed saddles were invented).

Flexibility is a wonderful quality that enables human beings to grow on a personal level as well as professionally.

Depth/Profoundness: Anyone seeking depth and profoundness can easily end up losing themselves and finding darkness and confusion that goes hand in hand with the unknown. This type of pursuit for depth can lead to bitterness, loneliness and sorrow.

There is another path to depth and profoundness: Joy. Lightness of being and humour will make the journey a lot easier and clearer for the person seeking it.

Horses seek depth in their human partners in a way that is connected with patience in order to grow, learn and expand. If loneliness, bitterness and sorrow are part of the human's search for depth, patience will not prevail. Nor will joy and happiness which is a strong energy that horses respond well to.

Honesty and Openness: Without this hugely important quality, horses will never recognize you as a leader, no matter how many times you push them in the round pen!

For human beings, honesty boils down to telling the truth about something as we see it, which is not necessarily the real truth, only our opinion of it. It is our own interpretation of the truth in a situation, based on what we believe and how far we are willing to go with it (openness).

For a horse, honesty is when human beings reveal themselves and their weaknesses to them, including the powerlessness. By trying to hide or deny our weaknesses, we are lying to ourselves as well as to our horses. The truth, once revealed and unleashed, offers freedom, relief and quietness inside, along with happiness and the confidence necessary to push forward and grow. This, the horse can relate to. Remember the old saying "the truth will set you free".

Modesty: This is another quality that has lost some of its true meaning over time. Humans often pair up modesty with "formal politeness".

From a horse's perspective, modesty is having the wisdom to recognize your true abilities. The source of our creation works through us in a unique way. We must comprehend where our abilities come from in order to humbly see them for what they are. True modesty is not a superficial, external state of being but rather humility and proud inner presence.

Stillness: I believe humans have forgotten how to be still. The popularity of activities such as yoga and meditation are reintroducing the art of being still. Stillness does not mean death nor does it mean "not moving". We are talking here about an inner tranquility, a stillness of the mind, that keeps us in the present moment.

For a horse, stillness is a way of being on a regular basis. They do not need to remind themselves to turn off their brains, breathe deeply and be still. Their natural ability to do so allows them to survive in the wild, being aware of their surroundings in a calm and peaceful way. Even in the middle of active confrontations with humans, horses know how to have a grounded and rooted spirit that remains steadfast and true to them. Horses recognize this quality when they see it in humans.

Courage: this quality is not about doing daring feats on top of a horse. That would be a human's ego-related way of considering something courageous when it really should be qualified as something else (the word "bravado" comes to mind!). Courage is not about being fearless but rather knowing how to overcome your fears and be willing to try.

A horse can recognize courage when they see that a human is putting aside their ego to be in the moment and go through with their line of thoughts, believing in what they are doing, feeling what is right. That, to a horse, is courage and leadership.

Joy: horses see this quality in a human when they are genuinely calm, serene, happy, and have a gentle disposition about them. These qualities reflect inner strength and power. A joyful person is one that horses will want to bond with. The true nature of the horse is peaceful, calm, serene and joyful!

Devotion: This quality can be very misleading. If you are seeking to be good, noble and selfless in order to prove your devotion to your horse you are on the wrong track. A horse's devotion to you is much more simple and unconditional than that. Devotion comes from pursuing what you truly and honestly believe in, without a hidden agenda. If you are doing just that, your horse will recognize it in you because it will vibrate in your inner energy. A person must be able to see themselves as part of creation, being who they are without trying so hard to be "good", which is ego-based. Devotion is effortless and humans need to believe that just being themselves is good enough.

All these definitions can be summarized in one: Authenticity. Have you ever seen a horse pretending to be better than he/she is? How about a horse that is uncertain about which path to walk in the field. Have you ever seen them standing there wondering "Mmm, I wonder which trail would be better for me to walk today?" Horses do not doubt themselves and they don't second guess their leaders either. They are true, authentic, and they don't pretend to be anything else. This might sound complicated but it is actually a very easy state of mind to be in. The hard part is to believe in it and embrace it on a daily basis.

By understanding these definitions, you are allowing yourself to see the world through the horses' eyes. Man's way is not necessarily the best and only way to see the world. This is a huge step towards growing as an enlightened human being.

THE ZONE

7

"Think of a horse as a river: it doesn't need to know where it comes from or where it's going. It just flows."

- B-A. King

Photo courtesy Hoof Print Publishing

One of the most important concepts that needs to be understood in the Relationship Riding technique is what I call "The Zone". It is a space that is created between two individuals or animals, human/horse combination, parent/child, etc. The Zone establishes boundaries that are vital to any healthy relationship based on trust, respect and honesty. This concept embraces and encourages the individuality of each person or animal, allowing each to be their true self without having to give up what they believe in for the sake of the relationship.

Let's start with applying the concept to two individuals.

Imagine two circles, one labelled "A" and the other "B". Each circle represents an individual as a whole, with their own values, beliefs, likes, dislikes, goals, plans, ambitions (or lack of), etc. When individual "A" meets individual "B", they start sharing common interest such as hobbies, activities, beliefs, values, goals, etc. As they share these common interests, they also overlap their circles, or "bubbles", and create a new space that we will call "C" (see diagram below). This space is dysfunctional where the dominant personality begins to exert control.

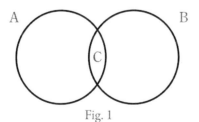

Fig. 1

Over a period of time, the "C" space will become more and more prominent as both individuals spend more time together. As the relationship continues, their common values, beliefs (spiritual, religious, education for their children, etc.) will also enlarge the "C" space. As this space becomes bigger and bigger, one of the individuals will lose their own personal bubble space (A or B circles), as they sacrifice their individuality to be part of the whole picture. The stronger individual will dominate the other and won't have to give up their personal bubble space. The dominant individual will continue to live their life based on what their preferences are while the submissive individual sacrifices and gives up many personal interests and beliefs. In the long run, the dominant individual takes over the relationship while the submissive individual blends into the values, beliefs, goals, etc established by the dominant one and loses their personal identity entirely. At this point, the submissive individual no longer has their own personal goals and interests since they are not taken into consideration and to try and have a voice becomes very difficult. That individual ends up becoming what the dominant individual wants them to be. This creates an imbalance within the relationship with the submissive individual losing who they intrinsically are. Unless the submissive individual reclaims their space/bubble entirely, the relationship will most probably fail or be permanently imbalanced.

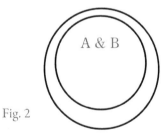

Fig. 2

The reason for this is quite simple: when we let our boundaries down (in this case our bubble space) we are allowing other individuals to manipulate our thoughts and wishes instead of respecting what we really want. Often, parents allow these types of sacrifices thinking that it is better for the family unit, since not everyone can have their own way. We also often see working parents put down their boundaries with their children because they feel they don't spend enough quality time with them and want to find a way to make it up. That is true, but there is another way around this situation without having to give up your "bubble" and individuality.

The "C" space is a direct result of a personal lack of respect. When we allow someone to "push" our bubble, either verbally, physically or emotionally, what we are really doing is lacking self-respect. We cannot command respect from others when we have none for ourselves. Keeping your bubble strong tells other individuals in your life that you stand for what you believe in and love yourself. This concept is especially important when dealing with children and teenagers. Teaching them self-respect while allowing other peoples' ideas and individuality is a life-skill that will come in very handy, helping them deal and identify bullying, manipulation and intimidation, at any age in their life.

Instead of creating a "C" space that will eventually envelope the submissive individual, it is better to create a new space that leaves each bubble or individual intact. I call this The Zone (see Fig. 3).

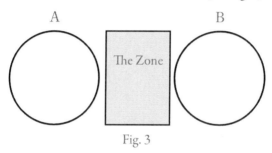

Fig. 3

In The Zone, individuals can share common interests, beliefs, hobbies, activities, views and opinions, etc. without jeopardizing their own individual being. The Zone can be a smaller or larger space depending on the individual's needs in the relationship (i.e. we may want more or less intimacy, emotionally or physically). They can agree to disagree and still be on happy terms, without one of the two feeling that they were forced into agreeing to something. It is difficult for parents to allow this type of relationship because as parents we believe that we know best and our children just have to believe that. Isn't that being dominant?

Wouldn't all of our relationships be a lot better off if we treated each other as equals and respected the other's space, opinions and values? Even with very young children, our role is not to dictate but to teach and learn. Even at a very tender age, children have a lot to teach adults with their childlike innocence. They have no reason not to trust and believe in the world. Adults teach children distrust as they grow up, along with how to lie, hide their true feelings in order not to get hurt and to not let their true colors show. What a shame that 10 or 15 years later these children will become adults that are searching for their true self and purpose, while they were born knowing it.

The Zone is applicable to all relationships in our life, including our horses. The herd members know how to move each other around without bursting their bubble or being disrespectful. For a horse, pushing another is only a way of finding out what position they hold in the herd, which means they know who their leader is. Also, they never let anyone burst their bubble out of respect for themselves and each other. When a horse is able to move another horse out of its way in a consistent manner, the submissive becomes lower in the pecking order. It's not a bad thing for a horse to be at the bottom of the hierarchy. It's just how it is. Horses that hold that position are very comfortable being there and because they are not natural leaders, they will let someone else do the job. They are still whole individuals with complete bubbles.

By standing up for your "bubble", in other words when you stay true to yourself and what you believe in and don't buy into someone else's ideas because they are "stronger" than you, what is really happening is you are respecting yourself as an individual. When you respect yourself, others around you will respect you too. It is very empowering for an individual to experience this and practise it with a horse.

Horses willingly show us the strength and weaknesses of our personal space, which we may not be aware of. Initially, in a gentle and subtle way, they will check our personal space by eating grass while we lead them out, push us with their heads while frisking us for treats, or use us as a scratching post. Their behaviour towards us will clearly indicate how strong our bubble is, and what our position in our human/horse herd is. It will eventually escalate to stepping on our feet, walking through our space, knocking us out of the way and even biting. When it comes to riding them, they will not respect us anymore than they did on the ground and more serious situations will occur when we start asking them to perform.

8

"Speed at the cost of quality is always wrong, not only in riding."

- Col. Alois Podhajsky

Photo courtesy Hoof Print Publishing

In this chapter, I use the word "training" for the purpose of understanding what we are talking about. I do not believe in "training" horses but rather in learning and teaching with them and from them.

Also, you will not need any fancy wand, stick, halter or other gimmick in order to work with your horse. All you need is an open mind, patience, and the will to learn. Also, you will need to be 100% authentic to yourself as well as to your horse (no hidden agendas here).

You might think this chapter doesn't apply to you because you bought a trained horse and all you have to do is get on and ride him. You might think that because you have absolutely no intention of becoming a horse trainer that you can skip reading this chapter all together. Training a horse happens every time you get on them, whether you are aware of it or not. Learning also happens every time you interact with your horse, even if you thought you weren't teaching or that you had nothing to learn from your horse. So you might want to read on, just for the sake of finding out what we mean by training, teaching and learning with horses.

First of all, it is good to know that each horse has his or her own unique learning abilities. Some of them will put up a terrible fight when learning to be tied but another aspect of training might come very easily to them. It is precisely for this reason that I don't have a specific plan already mapped out when I work with a horse. This is not a recipe. Also, please keep in mind that when a horse offers resistance, he is speaking to you. Whether you listen or not to what he has to say will determine whether your training is or is not successful.

First, I find out what the horse can already do and what is easy for him. This does not necessarily mean what he has been trained to do, but rather what this horse enjoys. Maybe bending is difficult because of a lack of flexibility or he has been ridden inverted and it is painful to move his body in certain ways. Maybe chasing him in a round pen is his favourite game. Whatever this horse enjoys doing, I play along with him and reward him passionately. Besides giving the horse confidence in himself, I am building our relationship, one moment at a time. I do not expect or demand results, I simply work hard at earning trust. This is no different than a relationship between humans.

Another very important aspect of learning is making sure the horse has every chance on his side to understand what I am trying to do with him. This is why I do not tie up horses when working with them. Horses are claustrophobic. If they feel "caught" and unable to get out of a situation, the only thing on their mind will be to escape, no matter what the consequence. They want to be free. By working with them at liberty the horse is free to run or move away from me when he feels too much pressure or is confused. In horse language, this means he is allowed to voice his opinion and leave an uncomfortable situation. If I am paying attention this is my cue to back off a little bit and listen to what my horse is trying to tell me. I will try a different approach in order to be clearer. When work at liberty is not possible, I use a lunge line and halter. Horses can still get away from me and move around, as long as I don't use the lunge line to tug his head and pull him back towards me. Again, a horse can pull away from me on a lunge line which is my indicator that I need to back off. This is often a good time to take a "breather", walk up to my horse and take a moment to pet him gently, listen to his breathing and allow him to process what is going on. I can then take a step back and slowly start over again. Although some people will think that I just rewarded my horse for doing the wrong thing, I actually encouraged him to communicate with me and I let him know I am willing to listen to his concerns. Isn't that what his leader does in the herd? Then, when I pick up from where we left off, the horse is usually happy to try again, knowing there is no threat.

Horses do not think like us. They process information differently and for different reasons. Their main line of thought is survival, on all counts, so their thought process goes along with that. That is why being a good leader to them is so important. In a horse's mind, a good leader represents survival.

By nature, horses are very respectful and compliant animals. They will give you warning signs before actually pushing, biting or kicking you. Humans, on the other hand, usually respond with a kick a lot quicker, with no warning sign. As a superior and intelligent specie is it necessary to over react with violence when something doesn't go as expected? If we pay attention to what the horse is saying from the very beginning, we wouldn't have to kick it in the first place. Think of a school yard brawl where one child kicks another:

"Why did you do that?" asks the teacher.

"He did it to me first!" replies the defensive child.

Where do you want to stand as a human being? Do you want to be stuck in the negative, violent reactions that only lead to more violence and no communication and comprehension? Or do you want to vibrate at a higher level of frequency/energy, one that allows you to capture and understand the subtle messages your horse is sending you? The messages are only subtle to us humans, they are very clear to horses. When a horse is resisting you, he usually has a very good reason to do so and it has nothing to do with being stubborn, bad, and stupid or any other negative adjective they are often labelled with. If we offer resistance when they are resisting us it will only escalate and we will get farther and farther apart. Although I am still talking about horse/human relationships, can you see the parallel between this situation and our relationships with our children, spouse, friends and co-workers?

Knowing the personality type of your horse will also help you in training him. This might sound goofy to some of you, but if you don't know how your horse learns, how do you expect to be successful at teaching him? Knowing your horse's personality type is not difficult. Basically, there are three types: leader, dominant and submissive. The majority of people I meet think there are only two types of personalities, dominant and submissive, simply because people think dominant horses are leaders. It comes as quite a surprise for some to know that dominant horses are not leaders and have no intention of being one. In the next chapter, we will take a better look at the different personality types.

Remember, this method is not a recipe or a series of games to be played until your horse is ready for the next level. You have to be in tune with your equine friend and expect to learn as much from him as he will from you if this relationship is going to work.

There is one thing you should keep in mind. Horses don't need you. They are born knowing everything they need to know in order to survive, including how to walk, trot, canter and gallop. They also know how to perform perfect flying lead changes, pirouettes and side passes. So what is it we are trying to *train* them to do? Nothing! We should only hope that they will be lenient enough towards us to show us how to ride these manoeuvres once we have learned how to ask for them properly, respectfully, and in a way the horse understands.

9

"Faith is believing without seeing."

- Unknown

Photo courtesy Hoof Print Publishing

I presume that horse personalities can be approached in many different ways, using a variety of categories, sub-categories and descriptions for all of them. We could probably end up with 25 to 30 different personality types. But, is it necessary to go that far in order to have a good idea of what our horse is really like? Do we really need to psycho-analyse our horses before we start working with them? Not in my opinion. I like to keep things simple, in harmony and easy for everyone.

I usually look at three different personality types based on herd dynamics, behaviour and psychology. Basically a herd is made up of a leader, dominant and submissive horses, as well as every other horse in between. Horses will usually fit in one of these categories, or fit in between two. Many people don't realize that a dominant horse is not necessarily a leader. The following is a brief description of each personality type to help you figure out who your horse is. Keep in mind that he may be a nice combination of dominant/submissive, or leader/dominant. Sometimes the herd is small enough to force the dominant to take over the role of leader, even if it's not something they want to do. If no other horse is able to be a leader that will keep them safe, then the dominant horse will do it.

The Leader

This personality type is pretty easy to pick out in a herd. He/she is the one that eats first and looks out for the herd. A leader's role in a herd is to find food and shelter for everyone and keep them safe. The herd all look up to the leader when they are uncertain about a situation. The leader will decide what the safest move to make is when there is danger in sight. The leader is usually very passive; they like harmony. In order for him to do his job, he needs everyone's attention and focus so that when the signal to run is given, the whole herd responds.

If two horses are fighting over something and not paying attention to their leader, they will miss what the leader is saying to them and even jeopardize the safety of the rest of the herd. Also, a leader cannot stay attentive and focussed on his environment when another horse, a dominant mare for example, is continuously bossing everyone around and creating chaos. A leader does need to rest during the day and the number 2 horse in the herd, the dominant, is usually the one that takes over leadership when necessary. The dominant horse often eats with the leader and follows him around pretty closely. It can actually be a little confusing sometimes to figure out who is the leader and who is the dominant. They sometimes switch roles during the day so it is not uncommon to see the dominant horse acting as a leader. If you are in doubt, throw out a flake of hay and see who eats first. Unless your leader is on vacation, he will most certainly be the first one to eat and will push anyone who got there quicker out of the way.

Some horse owners get confused because the horse they thought was the leader isn't always the first one to come in from the pasture or there seems to be another horse that is much lower in the pecking order that is allowed to eat with him. If a horse is a leader, why does it seem that other horses get privileges that are usually reserved to higher ranking horses? The answer is quite simple: leaders are confident in knowing who they are. When a horse asks another horse that is higher in the pecking order to share a meal, they do it nicely and respectfully (in horse language this means by not rudely pushing the other horse's personal space). More often than not, the higher ranking horse, which may or may not be the leader, will allow it. In my herd, it is not rare to see the lowest ranking horse eat out of the same hay pile as the lead horse. The other horses in the herd may want to put that horse back into their herd position if the leader lets them do so, but most of the time the other horses will carry on with their own meal and not worry about who is eating with whom. Always keep in mind that horses are very social animals and they enjoy each other's company. Their ego isn't threatened if a lower ranking horse needs the safety and comfort of the lead horse during the course of a meal.

The Dominant Horse

Most people refer to this horse as being bossy, arrogant and hard to handle at times because of their attitude. They also mistake this horse for the leader because of their very dominant nature. This might surprise some of you but the dominant horse does not want to be a leader. The dominant horse only wants to make sure that no one, absolutely no one, gets higher than them in the herd. They hold their position in the hierarchy very dearly. Most of the time, the dominant horse is number 2 in the herd. If the herd is very large and has sub-groups, a dominant horse will still have a position close to the leader. Dominant horses have no desire to be the leader but they also don't want anyone else to even think of taking their position. This is the horse that most often creates chaos and pushes all other horses around, especially the newer horses that have just joined the herd. The dominant horse will make sure that the newcomer knows exactly who the dominant one is and will keep reminding them on a regular basis ... just in case they forget! The leader will often have to remind the dominant horse that harmony is best kept in the herd for everyone's safety and happiness.

The Submissive Horse

This horse can be quite obvious to pick out in a herd. The submissive horse is at the bottom of the pecking order ... and very happy about it! Life is grand down there. Everyone worries about food, shelter and safety while the submissive horse just hangs out and follows everyone else around. When meals are served, he'll quietly take his spot, after everyone else, and eat his portion without trying to get extras, unless he gets permission. The submissive horse is rarely in a rush and he is often a horse that we consider "calm and bomb proof" because he has such a laid back demeanour. Many will qualify a submissive horse as lazy or stubborn. But this horse is far from it. Although more laid back, he is usually a happy-go-lucky type of horse with an independent streak in him. They are not easily impressed with humans dominating them (that's where they get labelled as stubborn) and will offer a lot of resistance to anyone trying to force a response out of them. The submissive horse rarely pushes another horse's personal space unless it is to verify it's position in the herd, and it usually does so with pinned ears or a head bob towards the other horse. It rarely starts cantering around the field to prove a point.

Interacting With Different Personality Types

There are horses that fit in between these categories. As we get to know our horse better, it becomes easier to know if they are more dominant or more submissive. They all have qualities from all three different personality types, but some traits will be more prominent and that is what will qualify them as being submissive, dominant or a leader.

As a horse owner it is important that you are aware of the type of horse you are dealing with in. You will then understand how your horse will react to your leadership and be empathetic to his reactions. What I mean by this is, for example, a submissive horse will refuse to move not because he is stubborn or lazy but because he is checking to see if you are a good leader. He would not refuse to move for his equine leader so that means you still need to prove to him that you are a leader to be trusted. Kicking, pulling, yelling and calling a submissive horse nasty names because you are frustrated with him will not help your case in proving that you are a good leader. Keep in mind that equine leaders are usually passive, calm and they promote harmony in a herd but they know their role and make it clear to all.

A horse with dominant traits will do everything in their power to make sure you do not have a higher position than them in the horse/human herd you create. This horse needs proof that you are a trustworthy leader that is patient, doesn't get mad, and provides food, water and shelter.

A horse with leadership qualities will be very happy to hand over the position to you if you prove to have the qualifications do to the job. But proving to a lead horse that you are a better leader than him takes time and patience. A horse's safety and survival lies in their "hooves".

One thing that seems to be overlooked in talking about horse personalities is that many factors can alter a horse's characteristics: age, size of the herd, gender, change in gender (gelding), life situations such as neglect, abuse, harsh training, their living conditions such as being isolated in a box stall or pasture living can also affect their temperament. For example, if your mare is dominant in her existing herd and you move her to another place, she will not automatically be dominant in her new herd. If the new herd is very big, the living conditions are different (pasture versus boxstall for example) and your mare is depressed and insecure because she misses her former herd, she might not act the same way. In time, she will most probably work her way back to the top of the herd into a dominant position, unless she is more comfortable being in a different position. Motherhood can also dramatically change a mare's personality.

Speaking of moving a horse to a new home, I am often asked how long it takes for a horse to adapt to their new environment. One week? Two weeks? A month? You might be surprised to know it takes one year. A horse needs to know that there is plenty of food, water and shelter during all seasons. These animals are genetically programmed to roam the land and find sufficient water and food in order to survive. Once a horse has seen all seasons in his new home and knows that there will be no lack of food, water and shelter, he can relax knowing all is well. This does not mean that we shouldn't move our horses nor does it mean that we should not do anything with them for a whole year once we have moved them to a new home. But we do need to take this knowledge into consideration. If you are in the position where you care for horses on a daily basis, observe how a new horse's personality changes over the course of a year. I have seen it time and time again with my own herd. After the one year mark, the "new" horse is calmer, more confident, easy going and seems to be relieved to know supplies are available year round. For an animal that strives on survival 24 hours a day, this is a good thing to know!

10

"It is the difficult horses that have the most to give you"

- Lendon Gray

Photo courtesy Louise Bolduc

In the previous chapter, we took a quick look at the three basic personality types in horses. It is important to remember that a horse's natural response is to follow his leader so no matter what category your horse falls under, they will respond to a good leader. A better way to approach this topic is to look at what the qualities of a good equine leader are.

One of the most important things to remember is that horses, as prey animals, have a very strong sense of their environment. This means they can pick up on energy sources that surround them and run away if anything seems threatening to them. A good example of this is to watch a herd of zebra grazing while a lion sleeps in the tall grass close by. As long as the lion's intentions are on sleeping and not eating, the zebras will know they are safe. As soon as the lion wakes up with hunger pains in his stomach, he will automatically start thinking about food, i.e. the zebras grazing close by. His thoughts will transmit energy/vibrations that will be "heard" by the zebras before the lion even has a chance to stretch.

When we approach our horses, they feel our energy and vibrations from far away. There is no need to be up close for them to pick up on what you are thinking and how you are feeling. So if you are thinking "this time you're not getting away from me, no matter what!" I can guarantee that your horse will be gone before you get a chance to hide the halter in your jacket. If you're thinking "I swear my horse can read my mind", well you're right! He can! This is where true leadership qualities come into play.

We can't fake our intentions with horses. You can't pretend to be happy when you're mad, you can't force gentleness when you truly despise the way your horse is reacting to you and you can't hide your impatience when they aren't doing "it" right (whatever "it" is that you are wanting them to do!). Your vibrational energy doesn't lie and that is what your horse is feeling from you, no matter how hard you try to wear your widest grin and fake it. Authenticity is your first step to being a good leader, one that your horse will believe and trust his life with.

A good leader doesn't get mad, lose his patience or yell. He also doesn't yank the shank, kick, push and throw things around. This doesn't mean that a good leader never loses it, but when they do they don't take it out on their horse. For example, if you are short tempered one day (and it happens to all of us, including me!) know that your horse will sense your tension and anger right away so you need to be extra careful in what you do and say. I usually suggest that you take a very deep breath (or ten!) and see if it improves your mood. Or, if you don't have to be with your horse at that moment, put him back in the pasture with his friends. You can then hang out with him and watch what they do together, or come back later. Leadership is very fragile and if we keep on acting poorly, it will take a lot of convincing to prove to our horse that we are worthy as a leader and deserve the responsibilities that go with it.

Horses are extremely tolerant and patient. That means it's okay for us to make mistakes and try again. You will lose your cool and you might even say nasty things to your horse at some point, but an apology and stepping back from the situation will carry you a long way. Horses understand more than we are willing to give them credit for. Always keep in mind that they really can read our minds/vibrational energy and they understand when we apologize, as long as it is genuine and authentic. Isn't this what true friendship is about? When our best friend blows up at us or doesn't return our calls because we've had a fall out, we automatically wipe the slate clean and start over when they genuinely apologize. It's no different with horses.

Working with your Leader Horse
If you own a leader horse, you are working with a horse that knows firsthand what it takes to be a good leader and the strict guidelines required. Lead horses will give up their leadership role, for the benefit of the herd, and let another horse be leader if they believe the other horse has the capabilities to do so. If you want his job, you will have to prove yourself to him. All it really takes is a lot of consistency and

some basic knowledge on horse leadership.

Your leader horse will want to see you as being very consistent in your leadership skills. He will test you in many ways to make sure that you know what your are doing. For example, he will push into your space (sometimes very subtly), which is often interpreted as your horse wanting to be close to you and hug you, maybe even looking for treats. Actually, a horse that approaches you and gets too close for comfort is testing your boundaries. If he is allowed, he will push you around with his head, make you back out of his space and even step on you if you stand too close. A horse can also push into your space in very, very subtle ways, like shifting his weight towards you without really moving his feet and pushing his belly into your bubble by turning his head away from you. He doesn't need to turn his head to see what is going on. His 180° vision on each side of his body allows him to see perfectly well without having to turn his head away from you.

One thing the leader gets to do in a herd is eat first. This really proves that he is the leader without any doubt. So, if you want to prove to your horse that you are the leader, DO NOT LET THEM EAT! Once he has the halter on there is no eating permitted. When a horse tries to eat while being ridden on the trail or led to the barn, what he is really doing is testing your leadership skills. In his mind, you can't possibly be a leader if you allow him to eat first and since I don't believe you have any intentions of munching the green grass under your feet, your horse should never be allowed to eat. This does not mean that you can't give him a treat after a good ride, as long as he takes it without stepping inside your boundaries. This will tell him that you can offer him food but you are still the leader and that he can't push you around for more treats.

Your leader horse will also have a hard time being focussed on you, probably watching his own herd and wondering when this human is going to leave him alone. You will have to be vigilant and always ask your horse to pay attention to you. If you were a horse, you would do this by moving abruptly in the opposite direction, pin your ears or do some similar action that would get the other horse's attention and focus. Because I am human and have the hardest time pinning my ears, I choose to snap my fingers or slap my leg to keep his attention. I also move quickly in the opposite direction of where the horse is standing.

I do this in order to create a space between us where he can turn in without pushing my bubble and have room for his own. Then I stand still for a few seconds and reward my horse by stroking his face gently. If I am saddling up or I'm in a position that will make it difficult to move abruptly in the opposite direction, I will snap my fingers. When my horse turns his head towards me, I acknowledge his attention and reward him with some loving before going back to whatever it is I was doing. The good news is convincing your horse that you really want to be the leader doesn't take very long if you are consistent in every move you make. Your leader horse will be so happy to know that someone wants his job since it is not an easy position to fulfil in the herd.

Working With Your Dominant Horse
Picking out the dominant horse in your herd is quite simple since it usually is the horse standing right beside the leader and is often a mare, as long as you have mares living with geldings in your herd.
Now that you have discovered that your horse holds the dominant position in the herd, don't worry, it's not as bad as it seems. Keep in mind that the only thing a dominant horse wants to be is, well, dominant! A dominant horse does not want to give up their position in the herd. They also don't want to be a leader which means when you halter them and create your little personal herd, someone needs to be a leader or the dominant horse will. They will test you, like all other horses, and they will probably test you a little more often, but the bottom line is they need a leader and if you prove to be a good one, they will embrace you for it.

Working With Your Submissive Horse
Many think that this is the easiest horse to work with. In my opinion, it is the hardest.

A submissive horse has a very laid back attitude. His way of testing your leadership is to say "make me" and that can be somewhat frustrating. For example, when doing ground work with a submissive horse, their focus is rarely on you, the wannabe human leader. They are focussed on their real equine leader and their herd, wondering where they are. In the herd, submissive horses do not worry about focussing on the leader at all times either since there are other horses doing that already. When the herd starts moving or running for safety then that is a good time to follow them. This also explains why submissive horses don't move very quickly, unless necessary. Most are not afraid of the cracking whip and will pretty much ignore any antics you will perform to make them go. The secret to working with a submissive horse is to be very, very patient because if you lose your cool, you automatically tell them what they already speculated: you are not a leader and if that horse could talk, you would hear him say "I knew it!" You must be able to make the submissive horse pay attention to you in order to make yourself believable as a leader. This means you will be snapping your fingers a lot and paying special attention to what they are doing behind your back. They will test your leadership when you are not focussed on them.

The "tone" of your silent voice, in other words your body language/ energy/thoughts, will be different with each personality type. A leader horse doesn't usually need to be "talked" to very loudly. They quickly understand what you are saying. That's why they are the selected leader for their herd. A dominant horse will need you to "speak" a little louder and firmer, using more energy in your body to make yourself convincing as a leader. The submissive horse will probably push you to the limit without using any form of physical violence until they completely disrespect you.

It is very important to remember that no matter what personality your horse is, he will always test your leadership in some way. It is a primal and basic survival instinct for a horse to know who is who in a herd. When you are with a horse, you must offer the same genuine equine leadership that they are used to in order for them to respond to you as they would to their equine leader.

Also, you can't just vote yourself in as a leader. You have to convince your horse that you have the capabilities of being one and the only way to do that is to believe you can. Authenticity will help you gain respect and trust from your horse and those are true qualities of a good leader. You must also follow the rules established by horses (not ours!):

Do not pull, tug, push or yank on their heads. It is the biggest form of disrespect towards a horse.

Do not let them eat unless you are offering it to them, allowing them to do so in a respectful manner without pushing or frisking you for more.

Do not let them push into your personal space.

DO listen to them and try to understand what they are telling you without labelling them as stupid, dumb, lazy, stubborn, etc., or by judging them in any way.

Your horse will fall into one of these categories and may also be a combination of two. Either way it's up to you to be the best leader you can be no matter what personality type your horse is. If you are an authentic leader he will respond to you. Also, don't compare him to your friend's horse who acts totally different with her. Each horse is as individual as each human being that graces this planet.

11

"Live in the spirit of blessing, not blaming".

- B-A King

Photo courtesy Hoof Print Publishing

I f you only read this chapter in the entire book and apply what is suggested, you will make a huge difference in your life as well as in your horse's.

This might sound too good to be true but there is one solution to all the behavioural problems that arise when working with your horse. Let me specify that if your horse has any medical problems you must have this checked out first. The solution I am about to propose to you will not do any good if your horse is in pain or if he is sick.

Leadership

I believe leadership is one of the most misunderstood concepts when working with horses. Most everyone knows that they have to be a leader for their horse but they don't know how to be an authentic leader based on horses' needs. Leadership does not mean who gets to boss whom around. When we want to be a good leader for our horse, we have to mimic the lead horse's behaviour and understand why he acts the way he does. He does not get mad, frustrated, lose his patience, or yell at his herd mates. As a good leader his job is to keep his herd safe and make sure everyone has food, water and shelter. When we feed a herd, we will often see the lead horse taste everyone's portion of hay. He's not being greedy, he's making sure that everyone has proper food and, most importantly, he is checking to make sure they all respect his leadership, even when there is food around. When a new horse is introduced to the herd, the lead horse will automatically push him out and gradually let him in if he respects the rules that are established by the leader. These rules are very simple: pay attention to the leader and don't create chaos amongst the rest of the herd. The reason for these rules is also very simple: if a horse is not paying attention to his leader because he is too busy messing around with another horse, he will miss the signal that says it is time to run for safety and in doing so he may jeopardize the whole herd's safety because of the distraction he caused.

A lead horse does not get mad at his herd mates and this earns him respect, trust and instils a sense of safety and security. Even when we see our leader violently chase, kick or bite another horse, he is not mad but simply re-establishing boundaries with this disrespectful horse. We need to do the same when interacting with our horses. Of course, it is sometimes impossible to not get frustrated and lose our patience, but instead of taking it out on your horse, walk away. I know this may seem controversial to many because you have been told to never let your horse win or else you lose his respect. Well, respect and trust has nothing to do with winning arguments! Compassion and understanding, on the other hand, will win you a lifelong friend. If you walk away and regroup yourself for a few minutes by taking some deep breaths (as many as necessary), you will have a clearer understanding of the situation and will be able to handle it with much more compassion and sensitivity. This is something your horse will understand. You can always re-address your issue when both of you have calmed down and relaxed a bit (my teenage students would say "chill" or "don't spazz" ...!). Something else to keep in mind is that horses do not process information the same way we do, nor do they process it at the same speed. We want immediate responses because we are very clear on what *we* want and understand the way we are asking it. Horses don't speak English and very often have no clue what we are asking. They do not have human brains and do not process information in the same way or for the same reasons we do. The ultimate question on their mind is always "Will I be safe?" So we must ask ourselves "are we being ambiguous, does the horse understand us?"

Besides respecting our and our horse's personal spaces at all times, we also have to be very vigilant on another level: Food. Notice how the lead horse is always the one that eats first. That means that in the herd that is created between you and your horse, the same rules apply (no, that does not mean you have to eat the hay!). What it does mean is that your horse *does not* get to eat at all if you are interacting with him as a leader (i.e. leading, grooming, riding, etc.). It is just basic herd dynamics. So all of you trail riders who allow their horses to munch on the trail as if it was an open buffet, or worse, think that their horse just does that because he is misbehaving and there is nothing you can do about it, think again. Your horse is testing your leadership abilities by eating. He does not do it because he is hungry. He just wants to know if he can, thus revealing if he is the leader or not. Your horse probably got away with this behaviour many times before and knows he will get away with it again. Your horse knows you have no personal boundaries when you are on his back, riding on the trail or where ever it is that he plunges to eat while you are with him. Also, if your horse goes for green grass as you lead him, he is again testing your leadership. The good news is this problem is very easily fixed. Just hold the lead rope a little tighter in your hands and be ready when your horse decides to eat. The moment he tries to "go for it", hold the lead rope tight (do not pull, just hold it tight). If he still manages to eat (they are very strong and this is likely to happen), then stomp your feet, make noise, do anything to get his attention and stop him from eating. This action will tell him that you are the leader and he is not to eat, but also tells him to pay attention to you, which is something horses have to do with their herd leaders. Be consistent with this. Never, ever, allow your horse to eat and you will soon see a big difference in him as you lead him around and ride him in green pastures.

"What about feeding treats? Does this mean we can't do that anymore?" you might ask. Of course not. I love treating my horses after riding and I even use treats during training on certain occasions. But, when I feed a treat to my horse I make sure he does not take one single step towards me in order to get more. I do not allow them to push my personal space at all while I offer them treats, one by one. Once this is established you will never have to deal with a pushy horse that frisks you for treats every time you are together. If you want to allow them to graze a little before returning them to their pasture/paddock/box stall, simply grab a handful of grass and offer it to them while crouched. Let him know you are allowing them to graze even if you are not eating it yourself. They truly understand this and will recognize the leadership in you. When you are done grazing, again don't pull on the shank. Instead, snap your fingers, kiss, slap your leg, anything to make his head pop up. Then lead him gently away. If he refuses and goes for the grass, make yourself "louder" with your stomping or slapping. With a very obstinate or challenging horse, you

can also slap his shoulder muscle with the back of your hand. This large muscled area is the spot of choice for a horse bite or kick. It is one of the "correctional" areas that horses use amongst themselves. The hindquarter is the other area but I don't suggest you stand at arm's length and slap their rear end unless you want to take the chance of being kicked. Do not make it a habit of slapping your horse on the shoulder. Use this only if all else fails and he is still challenging you.

I believe the most important aspects of showing our horse we are good leaders is to protect our personal space and not let them eat, unless we offer. If you only do these two things, you will already be a much better leader and you will see a huge difference in your relationship with your horse. Your time spent together will be much more enjoyable and everything you ask and do with your horse will be easier. Just imagine yourself sitting on your horse, in the middle of a lush green field where the grass is so high it tickles your horse's belly. You stop to admire the scenery and your horse does the same, without even thinking of going for the grass. This is a very attainable goal and you will achieve it once you have proven to your horse that you are a consistent leader for him.

Boundaries

What makes a horse a great leader? He has strong boundaries and is very aware of them, never abusing his power or taking for granted the trust and respect that he has earned from his herd mates. By the way, this is also what makes a great parent, teacher, spouse, manager, mentor, CEO ... person! When the lead horse establishes his boundaries and sticks to them, every other horse knows what to expect of him without any ambiguity. Oh they will test those boundaries, every day, many times a day, but if the leader is consistent then the inquisitive horse feels safe and happy knowing his leader is still on top of the game, keeping the herd safe. That is very reassuring for a prey animal that has absolutely no desire to be a leader in the first place, but will do the job if no one else has the ability to do so. In other words, your horse will test your boundaries regularly just to make sure that you are still the leader you were the last time he checked. He doesn't do this to get you mad, or because he is stupid, stubborn or lazy, but simply because he needs to know that you are a very good leader while trusting you with his life. With horses, it always comes down to survival, which is something we take for granted as humans since our survival is rarely in jeopardy. When you keep your boundaries up, you are respecting yourself. That is a sure way to be respected by others. Think about it for a minute; when you let your child or spouse get their way in a situation that they know you are adamantly against, you let your boundaries down and agree to let them push you or your beliefs. Women have a tendency to do this a lot because they want to keep the peace within the family and make everyone happy ... except themselves. In the long run, those women pay a dear price for allowing their family members to push their boundaries. Luckily for them, there are some fabulous horses out there willing to teach them all about boundaries and how to get back their personal space. Weak boundaries are also the basis for bullying. When a bully knows that he can get what he wants with you, he will keep doing it until you raise your boundaries and make them strong. Suddenly, bullying you is not so much fun anymore. By the way, bullies are not only found on the school ground but also in teacher's lounges, at home and work places. We just give it another name when it involves adults: harassment. When you are consistent with your boundaries, people around you will catch on quick, especially children, but they will check in on you regularly to make sure that you are still a strong leader, one they can count on. A lead horse is consistent and if he is not up to the job one day, the number 2 horse will step in and take over for him.

Horses trust their leaders. If the lead horse jumps over a running creek because it is safer on the other side, the others will follow. No matter what he asks of them, they will follow because he has proven to them that he can be trusted and that he respects and trusts them. It is no different for us when we establish ourselves as a leader for our horse. If we do a good job and prove to them that we are consistent, caring and trusting leaders, they will not spook when we introduce them to something new. They will trust us when we ask them to go on a new trail and they won't be terrified or reluctant when we try to handle their feet. I work with many abused horses and once I establish myself as their leader, and they accept me as a leader, I am able to touch the ears of very head shy horses, hold them for the veterinarian without having outbursts of panic, saddle and ride them without any bucking or run away incidents. But, I absolutely must be a true leader, one that does not demand anything from my horse but asks instead. If I don't get what I asked for, I don't get mad or lose my patience. I will take a good look at myself and examine how I am asking and if it is clear to the horse, not just me. I will also either express myself in a different way to help the horse understand what I am looking for or I will take a step back to take the pressure off and let him think about things as he chills out. Another option is to do something that is easy for him to understand, something he already does well and enjoys doing. This will build his confidence either way and confirm my position as a trustworthy leader. It is not about demanding and reprimanding, but all about teaching and repeating (by the way, this works wonderfully well on children and teenagers also. Bonus!).

You Can't Hide Your Emotions
As prey animals, horses are very sensitive to the energetic vibrations in their environment. That is how prey animals manage to get away from predators. When we have the wrong attitude within our vibrational energy field and approach a horse, they will probably walk away from us or stand in fear of what we are going to do to them. They can feel your energy from a hundred feet away (maybe more!). Horses live in the moment and that's the best place to be with them.

It is not easy to be a good leader. We have to work on our patience and tolerance, be aware of the horse's body language on a continuous basis, and always have the right attitude. Luckily, horses are probably the most tolerant animal around and they are very good teachers. They will quickly let us know when we are not being a good leader by leaving our side or pushing our boundaries. We also need to keep in mind that it is normal for a horse to test our leadership several times a day. This is not done in order to get us ticked off. It is simply their way of making sure we truly are great leaders and we can keep them safe, fed and happy. Taking on leadership is a big responsibility (no wonder horses don't want to be leaders) and we need to be aware of all the implications if we seriously want to do this correctly. Some things to consider are: learning how to be aware of our emotions since they vibrate in our energy field (i.e. physical and verbal reactions) as well as not taking the horse's reaction to our leadership skills personally.

There is no room for ego in a relationship between mankind and animal. Actually I don't believe there is any room for ego in any relationship! Ego will only get in the way of your true-self and build up tension between you and your horse (or anyone else). Too many times I have seen horses being at the receiving end of a bruised ego and that simply is unfair and certainly not a way to build a trusting relationship. Recently, I witnessed a young local rider attending a high-end jumping competition. The crowd was excited to see this young rider perform and I'm certain she was also very nervous about performing for her home town crowd. She entered the riding ring on a beautiful, promising horse that was obviously well trained and ready for this competition. As she approached her very first jump, her horse slammed on the brakes at the last minute and sent his young rider flying. Luckily, she did not hurt herself, but she did get a very big bruise on her ego. Unfortunately, her horse got the raw end of the stick (literally!) and paid dearly for her bruised ego. He got severely cropped on his rear end as she rode him out of the ring. No need to say the crowd was silent and disappointed in this promising rider. No one wants to see animals beaten for not performing. It only proves that there is a huge lack of maturity on the rider's behalf as well as a lack of understanding.

As a good leader it is up to us to convince the horse that what we are asking of them is safe AND in exchange we must listen to their response. Good leaders always listen to what their team mates have to say. If the horse refuses to perform, they most probably don't understand what we want of them and/or they don't trust us and/or they don't like doing it. Not every horse wants to be a jumper, even if top dollars were spent on him and his pedigree says he should be successful. Inflicting pain on them through harsh hands at the other end of a bit, spurring or cropping will not make the situation any better. No wonder some horses are hard to catch, saddle and bridle. They know what's coming and if by any chance their owner is in a rush that day and their vibrational energy is not a very calm one, they will know what to expect from the upcoming training session and will most probably do everything to get away from you. The Relationship Riding philosophy espouses that a horse responds to you through willingness and trust, not through pain, fear or discomfort.

Good leadership will take you far ... very far! I have experienced firsthand the results of being a good leader to the horses I work with. Many of these horses are in remedial training and gaining their trust and respect by showing them I can be their leader is crucial for growth. For these horses, if I was to inflict any kind of fear, pain or discomfort, I would not be able to do anything with them safely. These horses often no longer have any trust or respect towards humans and their beautiful spirits are often crushed because of abuse. Imagine trying your hardest to please your owner and as you are about to jump over a fence, the rider tightens up, hurts your mouth with the bit and throws you off balance. You stop to keep yourself and your rider safe and in exchange you get a good beating for it. Confusing? I would say! A simpler example is when a horse owner tries to catch their horse and is in a hurry to do it. The horse gets away from them and gives them a run for their money. Eventually, the owner succeeds in catching the unruly horse and as soon as the halter goes on, the yank-the-shank action starts, painfully hurting the tender area behind the horse's ears as the owner punishes the horse for making them run around. Next time, I can bet that the horse will run a little longer to avoid this kind of pain. Wouldn't you?

Being a good leader is not about being perfect and knowing everything there is to know about horses. I still learn from them every day (as well as from my students) and I have been at it for 35+ years. But the one thing you must have is a good attitude and be willing to treat your horse with at least as much respect as you would someone that is dear to you, whether it be a friend, spouse, child, etc. Learn the rules to good leadership and you will be successful with all horses you encounter. Your personal life will probably benefit also.

BITLESS BRIDLES AND TREELESS SADDLES

12

*"Knowledge will keep you free from the desire
to dominate through fear."*

- Author unknown

Photo courtesy Hoof Print Publishing

W hy ride without a bit? I guess the real question is "Why ride with one?"

Horses were ridden by man without the use of a bit and treed saddle for centuries. If we are to stay in the mindset of doing things that are natural to a horse, treeless saddles and bitless bridles are just common sense. But common sense can be something that is difficult to adhere to when there are traditions engrained in our training methods. Most of us don't even know why, when and how we started using bits and treed saddles, thinking they have always existed. Riding horses without a bit asks the human to invest time, trust, respect and love into a relationship with an equine. When time, trust, respect and love come in small doses or run out, humans need to find other ways of getting what they want. Using pain, fear or discomfort with tools usually gets quick, effective results so it becomes acceptable (unfortunately not only with horses but also with children and captive animals). Humans see themselves as being above and beyond every other creature. By doing so, this allows humans to deny that there is any type of intelligence, love or joy in animals, giving humans the secure sense that no animal is suffering at their expense. If humans were to accept that animals have intelligence, feel love and joy, fear and pain, that would ask us to consciously revise how we treat the animals in our lives. That is an emotional responsibility that many are unwilling to accept. So, I expect humans will resist this as long as possible: it is much easier than admitting we are causing mental, emotional, intellectual and physical problems to our horses. I believe in the goodness of mankind and I feel a shift in consciousness every time I get an opportunity to speak to open minded people about their relationship with their horses.

Keep in mind that a horse's ability to move is extremely important to them, more so than anything else. Having the ability to run, kick up their heals, play with each other without being restrained by space makes up their entire essence. A horse expresses himself through movement.

I believe knowledge is a powerful tool and when researching how riding horses all began, I discovered the use, and non-use, of treed saddles and bitless bridles.

A Little "Bit" of History (pun intended!)

Even when they were first invented, bits were meant to exert control by using pain and/or fear to the horse. That's how and why they worked. This explains why the ridden horses, in ancient art works, had open mouths and a body posture that was a result of a constant battle to avoid the pain caused by the bit. Bits are no different today. We have designed softer versions of bits in the hope of being more gentle, but we have also designed some very harsh bits. Gadgets have been invented to close the horses' mouths (which makes for nicer artwork!) but the cause and effect are the same.

There are strong ligaments, called nuchal and supraspinous that run from the horse's poll all the way to the tail. When the horse lowers his head, the nuchal and supraspinous ligaments which are located in the poll/neck and whithers/back area are pulled tighter in order to support the horse's back. This tightening of ligaments also keeps the vertebrae beneath them in alignment and allows good transference of impulsion from the quarters through to the forehand. Conversely, when the horse's head is up, these ligaments slacken and the spine is less supported. This will also cause dipping in the horse's back, resulting in an inverted horse.

During bone pathology investigations on horses from burials in the Ukraine and the Altai, dating around the 1st millennium BCE, abnormalities in the caudal thoracic vertebrae were discovered. Historians believed that such wear on the vertebrae were because of the use of severe bits, causing horses to have an inverted posture when ridden to avoid the pain and discomfort in their mouths.

As far as saddles go, all treed saddles are designed to do the impossible, which is to fit together a human and a horse by putting a hard platform between them. The humans seat will fit properly when using the right size saddle, but a horse's body shape and condition will vary a lot throughout the year. So even if the saddle is custom fitted to a stationary horse, the horse's shape will change with movement and no longer fit the minute we start riding them. When a horse is in motion, their backs move like a wave. The ligaments on the horse's back tighten and slacken, as mentioned above. A human's body is flexible, the pelvis also having the ability to sway back and forth. When the two bodies, human and equine, move together, there is no point of pressure, just beautiful flowing energy in motion. Stick a hard tree between the two and the whole dynamics of movement change.

That being said, there were still warrior groups such as the Celtic Irish Chieftain Finn MacCumhail's Fianna that disapproved the use of bit and saddle, riding with their skills and the horse's forbearance alone.

"If he will consent to bear you, bear you he does; and if not, well, no bit, bridle, whip or thong will tame him."

– Lord of the Rings, JRR Tolkien

Bitless Bridles
There is a lot of scientific research, for those who need that extra convincing, that proves without a doubt that metal in a horse's mouth is detrimental to a horse's health. Besides causing negative physical effects, bits also create a lot of behavioural issues that could be easily resolved if it was removed. Here are a few examples:
- Anxious, unpredictable, nervous, scared, spooky, panicky, tense, stressed behaviour
- Difficult to slow down or stop, bolting or rushing
- Resistant, aggressive, cranky, angry, confrontational, mean
- Head shaking, tossing and flipping
- Horse is difficult to catch, bridle (on and off), standoffish, pins ears, bites or threatens to
- Running wild on a lunge line, fidgety and tense when mounting, neck braced, rearing up
- Stiff or choppy strides, busy mouth (fussing with the bit), refuses to jump, difficulty in travelling in a straight line (drifting)

- Unfocussed, salivates excessively
- Stumbles for no apparent reason, hollows its back, tries to bite reins, refuses to stand still
- Rubbing muzzle or face on forelegs, head shyness, difficult to handle around ears and/or forelock.

A horse that has behavioural issues such as these cannot learn to concentrate on the rider and will spend time focussing in a counter-productive way on the bit and the pain it causes. This will lead to the horse trying to find ways to get rid of the bit, and even the rider, in order to get away from the pain. A horse can pay much better attention to the rider and enjoy what they are doing together when it is not dealing with pain, fear or discomfort. Horses are not lazy, stupid, stubborn, etc. They actually are curious, love to play, are good natured and ready for new adventures when they are treated properly and have the proper leadership. If they are not being the ideal riding partner that you are looking for, you need to take a look at what you are doing to them, not the other way around.

The bit is not necessary in order to have proper communication with a horse. A good rider will communicate very effectively with his horse using his seat, body and intentions. The rider must be willing to invest time with their horse in order to develop a strong relationship based on good leadership and better communication without diverting to the use of aids such as spurs, crops, tie-downs, hard hands and legs. Remember that horses communicate on three levels: body language, vibrational energy and telepathy. The rider must also be ready and willing to work on his riding skills every time he mounts his horse. I have been riding horses my whole life and I work even harder at being a good rider today than I ever have. I am more conscious of what my body is telling my horse and how my horse is reacting to my movements. My goal is always to be the best rider I can be for my horses, and that often means going around in the arena at a walk, focussing on my breathing, the softness in my body and how my horse feels about it all, before doing anything else. That's the least I can do for a friend that graciously allows me to climb on their back and enjoy the exhilaration of riding them.

There are many different types of bitless bridles on the market today but not many offer a different concept. Basically, these bridles put pressure on and around the horse's head, nose or jaw to "encourage" direction. At least, that is what we choose to see as humans, that we are encouraging direction and not forcing it on the horse. One of the most important rules of the Relationship Riding philosophy is to leave the horse's head alone. Horses do not like to have anyone push, pull, yank or squeeze their heads. To them, this is very rude because we are pushing into their personal space. We don't let them do it to us so why do we think it would be acceptable for horses to have us do it to them? When we do this, we automatically lose their trust and respect. Take a few minutes to observe horses playing together, or even herding one another around. They do not push or pull on each other's heads. Instead, they put pressure on their herd mate's body (belly, shoulders and hind quarters), getting them to move out of the way. Naturally, the more convincing leader of the two will succeed in doing this.

A Closer Look at Bitless Bridles

You have probably heard of the hackamore and bosal, two of the most popular bitless head gears available on the market. What you might not know is how and why they work so well.

Hackamore: this device relies on leverage for efficacy. The hard nose band is made of rubber-covered motorcycle chain or saw-toothed *serreta* which was used by traditional Andalusian Vaqueros. It is in direct contact with a very sensitive area on the horse's nose. The curb-chain also creates pain in the chin groove when pressure is applied to the reins. The double action pain that occurs simultaneously is sure to stop any horse. It can also cause separation of the vertebrae at the top of the neck and can break the bridge of a horse's nose.

Bosal: a gentler form of hackamore, this device is a simple loop made of rawhide. The fit of this loop is very important: too small will create sores and too large will slip up the face. With the reins attached to the back of the loop, they are used essentially for stopping or downward transitions by pulling the bosal down onto the nose via the reins. The reason this works is because of the pain created on the bridge of the horse's nose.

Side-Pull: this bridle looks very much like an English-type bridle without a bit. Reins are attached to the rings on each side. Usually the nose band fits loosely, which can create sores on the nose and does not allow for a clear line of communication. Also, most riders do not position the noseband high enough which puts too much pressure on the softer, sensitive area on the horse's nose. The direct rein pull not only aggravates the horse (in horse language this means lack of respect) but also encourages him to get into a pulling match with you. Honestly, I don't want to wrestle with a 1000 lb animal. Do you?

Rope halters: these were popularized by the natural horsemanship movement. It has to sit loosely on the horse's face or else it will be quite uncomfortable, especially at the poll and nose area. Even when it is fitted snugly, there is a lot of movement and rubbing against the horse's face because it is used like a side-pull.

Pressure halters: the most popular of these models looks like a regular halter that has a cord with rings at each extremity, positioned below the nose band. The reins attach to the rings. When pulling on a ring, the cord tightens around the horse's nose. They are primarily intended for schooling on the ground. They work because of the pressure that is put on the horse's sensitive nose area.

When using any of these bitless bridles, riders should learn how to ride without pulling the horse's head around. Even neck reining pushes into the horse's personal head space (the neck is part of the sensitive head space we need to learn to respect). Neck reining is a cued response, not a natural one. This means you have to teach the horse to give you the desired behavioural response.

Ideally, bitless bridles should offer the same leadership when riding as on the ground, without using any pain, fear or discomfort. The bitless bridle should not force the horse to obey what we want but instead suggest the direction we want to go. This is not done by using rein pressure, but rather by using the rider's body, including his hands. The good use of a bitless bridle depends a lot on how well the rider communicates to his horse and on how good a leader his horse sees him. A horse will always follow the direction offered by his leader because he knows he will be safe with him.

Relationship Riding Bitless Bridle: this bridle was designed with the Relationship Riding philosophy in mind. It causes no pain, fear and discomfort. It creates clear communication to the horse because of its well adjusted, comfortable fit.

Not all horses will respond well to the Relationship Riding bitless bridle when it is used for the first time. Some horses have been pulled and yanked on so much their mouths are hardened and they no longer feel anything, except the frustration of having their personal space disrespectfully invaded by the human on their back. For these horses, transitioning to a Relationship Riding bitless bridle may be a little slower because of the horse's distrust. Although the metal will not be in their mouths, they will still resist any pulling action coming from the rider. Relationship Riding mitigates this difficult transition by establishing the leadership and respect that is necessary for a good, safe relationship. This work is initially established on the ground. Setting the boundaries is important in riding in a Relationship Riding bitless bridle. Because we are not causing any pain, fear or discomfort, it is important that the horse knows that he cannot push against our personal boundaries, i.e. our hands or legs. When we have contact with our horse's head through the reins and we block our hands and pelvis to stop the forward movement (no pulling!), our horse will respond to this if he respects our boundaries. There is no use trying to ride bitless if you let your horse push you around. His behaviour will not change because you decided to be nice to him and take the bit out of his mouth. But it will change when he realizes that you are a true leader and that you don't cause him any pain for no apparent reason, which is what true leaders do. If you think that you are a wonderful leader for your horse but you are using a bit, think again. True leaders, as seen through the eyes and mind of a horse, do not create pain, fear or discomfort unnecessarily.

I have yet to come across a horse that cannot be ridden in a bitless bridle and I have rehabilitated many horses over the years, including runaways and the famous unstoppable horses. I have never used a bit on them.

Treeless Saddles

It would seem that riding without a tree in a saddle goes back at least as far as 1000 years ago. The Italian cowboys of long ago used a saddle they called Bardella. It was made out of cushions and stuffing materials such as straw. In those days, herdsmen rode for days, travelling much longer distances in the saddle than we normally do. Because the saddle was treeless, this allowed the horse's back to move freely, thus using all his dorsal muscles and keeping his back strong and healthy. A strong back allowed the horse to carry his rider comfortably and for a long period of time. Without the use of a bit or points of pressure from an ill-fitting treed saddle, the horse's head was down, allowing the nuchal and supraspinous ligaments to tighten, thus doing their job properly, as described earlier. The treeless saddle allowed the rider to follow the horse's movements. Therefore, in a treeless saddle, weight distribution does not become an issue since both the horse and rider are continuously moving together as one. The horse does not feel like there is a dead weight on his back that needs to be distributed along the panels of a tree for comfort.

There are many models of treeless saddles on the market. Most of them have a hard component in the pommel and/or cantle area. Keep in mind that whenever there is a hard part to a saddle, there is a risk of having points of pressure, especially in the whither and shoulder area. Ideally, try out the saddle on your horse before committing to buying one. Any serious saddle dealer will have no problem sending you a demo saddle to try out. Trust your horse's response when you try out the saddle. Even treeless saddles can be uncomfortable when they do not fit properly.

BIGGEST HUMAN MISTAKES

13

"The Point of Power is always in the present moment".

- Louise Hays

Photo courtesy Hoof Print Publishing

This chapter was inspired by a dear friend who so wants her and her horse to get along and, without realizing it, she sabotages her every effort. Thank you for reminding me that many people make the very same mistake. Hopefully, this chapter will enlighten us a little and help us understand our horses a little better.

As you are walking out the door, grabbing your halter and lunge whip, making your way to your horse in the pasture, you are suddenly bombarded with questions in your mind about what you are going to do with your horse today. "Should I be firmer, stronger without being aggressive? Should I back off? Maybe I'm scary and that's why he always runs away from me. Will I be able to catch my horse easily today? What am I doing wrong? Why is my horse good one day and not the next? I think I'll ride today. Well, maybe not, we'll see how he is."

Do you recognize yourself here? If so, you are committing one of the biggest human mistakes when dealing with horses.

Horses do not understand ambiguity. They live in the present moment. It is a question of survival for them. If a horse started questioning the reason and purpose behind why his leader is asking him to move *now*, some wouldn't live long enough to get an answer if they were living in the wild, surrounded by predators. Ambiguity equals confusion. When we try to convince our horses that we are great leaders for them and then turn around and question ourselves in their presence, do you really think they take us seriously? While you are dealing with everything going on in your head, your horse will turn around and leave, making sure you can clearly see his back end. This gesture in horse language clearly denotes a lack of respect/trust towards you. We must have a clear mind before undertaking anything with our horses. This explains why being in the present moment is so important to them.

You can't do anything about the past, it's gone. You can't do much about the future either because it doesn't exist yet. So the only thing that really matters is the present moment. Past and future ideas are useless to horses. We should try to adopt the same way of thinking, at least when we are interacting with them. If we wish to attain a close understanding and clear communication with our horses, we must be in the present moment with them.

This leads to human agendas. Wondering what we are going to do with our horse today, or, having it all planned out to the exact detail, all happens in our conscious mind. We may want to believe that we are not being dominant with our horses, but if we have a plan, no matter how big or small it may be, and we carry it out without even "asking" our horse how they feel about it, then we are being dominant, expecting the horse to be subservient. You do not have to be a psychic to know how your horse is feeling. Instinctively, I believe that every horse owner who truly loves their horse has either heard it's voice, or knew how it felt in a precise moment. That was because the horse was letting you know. For those of you brave enough to listen and reply back, you probably took your relationship to a higher level. For those who think "Humbug! I'll call the shots here.", you have probably been thrown off, kicked and/or bitten more times than others. Whether you are a professional trainer or someone who owns a horse in your backyard, you will avoid accidents and being hurt if you listen to how your horse feels. I developed a method of starting and re-starting horses called A.C.T. which stands for Authentic Colt Training. It is not based on what humans think a horse has to know before it is ridden. It is based on showing the horse what your intentions are and asking if they are willing to go along with it. Everything is done slowly in order to let the horse have its word and process the information presented to them. Also, only predators act quickly. They need to experience having tack on and carrying a rider at their own pace, without being forced into submission. We must leave our agendas behind. For these reasons, I never teach a colt starting clinic over a weekend, where participants come in with an unbroken horse and leave two days later riding them. First of all, I refuse to start riding horses that are younger than 4 years of age simply because their bones are too soft, not fully developed and it practically guarantees they will have premature ailments down the road (i.e. arthritis, separation of dorsal vertebrae, bowed tendons, etc). This eliminates a lot of potential participants wanting to attend such a clinic. Secondly, no two horses will learn at the same rhythm and to push them to follow the group is unfair. The third reason is the same as the second except it applies to humans. Clinics can be somewhat embarrassing when the clinician picks on you because you are the only one whose horse is not doing what everybody else's is.

When I start or re-start a horse, I rarely experience any bucking or erratic behaviour. If it does happen, then I need to back off and apologize to that horse for pushing it too hard. That usually ends the training session and I spend a lot of time making it up to them by grooming them, rubbing them in their favourite spot, making sure I am still a good leader by protecting my personal space and respecting theirs. My leadership has to be established all over again because I created either pain, fear or discomfort to that horse with no apparent reason to them. A real horse leader does not push its herd mates into a state of panic and fear based on dominance and expectations.

They Know What We Are Thinking

Horses don't have to speak English in order to know what we are thinking. They know simply by reading our minds (telepathy). When we enter a field with the goal of catching that *?!*#! horse, he will leave and stay away from you. Why in the world would he come up and be friendly to someone that thinks that of him? If you don't believe me, then here's a challenge for you.

Go to the field without any intentions of catching your horse but do bring your halter with you. As you are walking towards him, send him some love and apologize for not listening to him, for calling him names, and for losing your patience with him. Let him know that you just want to come up and say "Hi", giving him some love and touching his soft body. If he wants to walk away as you are approaching, stop and ask him permission to approach. Tell him again that you apologize and that you love him dearly, that you only want to get close to touch him and love him. Keep in mind that your horse can read your mind and your heart. If you are not sincere or authentic, this will not work. So don't blame your horse (or me!) if you don't succeed. Instead, look at your inner-self to see if you are in the present moment and being real. Maybe you were already thinking of how you were going to halter him? The goal of this exercise is to ask your horse if it's okay to approach him, then put his halter on if he agrees, and walk away peacefully together.

If you only succeed in getting close and petting him, that's great. If your horse trusts you and allows you to halter him, that's wonderful. If not, it doesn't matter. The point of this exercise is having no agenda, being in the moment, and letting the situation unfold as it needs to.

It is important to walk away from the situation if you start getting impatient and frustrated. That would only prove that you do have an agenda by not having your expectations met, thus being frustrated. That being said, you do want your horse to acknowledge you before you walk away. Even if you can't walk up to him and touch him, if your horse has stopped and faced you, he has acknowledged you and it's now okay to leave and try again later. You will be leaving the horse some food for thought along with the idea that you respected his wishes. That alone builds a very strong bond and relationship between the two of you.

The biggest human mistake is to assume that our horses don't know what we are thinking. Because they don't always comply with our demands, and some have very good reasons not to, we think they need to be taught how to move, how to use their bodies, how to live, etc. We presume they need to wear clothes, shoes and live in houses because we do. I've heard many people say that we should never give the horse an opportunity to discover that they are stronger than we are. Many people hurt horses and scare them to make sure they have control over them (dominance). Think about that last sentence, isn't it ironic?

I had an "a-ha" moment after reading a passage in Margrit Coates' book "Connecting With Horses". She was talking to a horse and the horse told her:

"Know who you are and be who you are. We are the spirit of love ... that is at the heart of each lesson that we offer".

This made me realize that horses want to not only offer lessons of love, but also lessons of self-love. By pushing our personal space on a regular basis, horses want us to realize that by keeping strong personal boundaries, we are respecting who we are, thus loving ourselves.

I can tell you without a doubt that every single horse owner out there is standing in front of a special teacher. Horses pick their owners. They also choose to live or die. They understand that death doesn't exist, they only leave their bodies and move on. I believe that horses' biggest wish is for humans to start listening to them telepathically, like they used to many, many years ago, and believe in the "magic" that is happening right before your eyes.

CONCLUSION

"You have come here to find what you already have."

- Buddhist Aphorism

Photo courtesy Hoof Print Publishing

I see horses, on a regular basis, being physically abused with traditional riding methods. I see horses being spurred until their flanks bleed, in the hope that they will become the next champion in their discipline and make their owners/breeders/trainers more prosperous. After so many years of seeing this happening first hand, you think I would get used to it, but I don't. If anything, I find it harder and harder to witness every time. My first reaction is to hurt that person as much as they have hurt the horse, but that would be irrational (and illegal!). For everyone's sake, including the horse's, I choose to focus on helping horse owners by teaching the Relationship Riding method. I choose to lead by example rather than being banned from stepping foot on a property for inappropriately "spurring" a cowboy/girl that hurt a horse. This way, I can help more horses than just the one that got me out there in the first place and hope that it will make a difference somewhere down the line.

My wish is that after reading this book you will now have a different way of looking at your horse. Maybe, one day, everyone will learn the real reasons why horses are part of our lives, which is to teach us and heal us. Maybe, one day, all horses will be loved and respected as they should. Maybe, one day, we can all make a difference, one horse at a time.

Maybe this is just wishful thinking, but I am going to keep on wishing. Will you join me in making a difference?

BOOKS

Communicating With Horses and *Horses Talking* by Margrit Coates
Horses: From Our Side of the Fence by Sandy Lagno
The Tao of Equus and *Riding Between the Worlds* by Linda Kohanov
Horsemanship Through Life by Mark Rashid
The Art of Horsemanship by Xenophon
How The Horse Has Shaped Civilization by J. Edward Chamberlin
Beyond the Mirrors: The Study of the Mental and Spiritual Aspects of Horsemanship by Jill Keiser Hassler
Horse Sense and the Human Heart and *Horses and The Mystical Path* by Adele Von Rüst McCormick, PH.D, Marlena Deboral McCormick, PH. D. and Thomas E. McCormick, M.D.
Animals in Translation: Using the Mysteries of Autism to Decode Animal Behavior by Temple Grandin
My Horses My Teachers by Alois Podhajsky
Talking With Horses by Henry Black
Dancing With Horses by Klaus Ferdinand Hempfling
The Ultimate Horse Behavior and Training Book by Linda Tellington Jones
The Power of Now by Eckart Tolle
La method Gentili by Bino Jacopo Gentili and Maria Franchini

WEBSITES

www.equine-behavior.com
www.torsion-scotland.com/history

Photo courtesy Kassia S. King

ABOUT THE AUTHOR
Barbra-Ann King
Founder of the Relationship Riding method

Barbra-Ann King started her journey with horses over thirty years ago. As the years passed, using traditional riding and training methods, Barbra-Ann came to the realization that there had to be a better way of riding than what she was experiencing with horses. Motivated by her passion to communicate with horses and in order to improve her relationship with them, she studied Horse Psychology and Behavior, Equine Sports Massage Therapy, Hands On Healing as well as the use of riding principles based on techniques that are centuries old. Eventually, she moved her practise to Cochrane, Alberta where she founded the Relationship Riding method.

Barbra-Ann lives by her mission statement: *"Bringing horses and people together, using no pain, fear or discomfort to the horse"*. Her passion for her work is contagious and she has turned many traditionalists into open-minded horse handlers. She has worked in therapeutic riding programs and was part of the Calgary Police Community Youth Wranglers program. Her various programs include *"EASI: Equine Assisted Self-Improvement"*, *"Women's Journey of Self-Discovery on Horseback"*, *"Youth Program for At-Risk Teens"* as well as corporate workshops including Leadership and Teambuilding Skills.

During her specialized workshops, private lessons and weekend retreats, Barbra-Ann expands the reach of the Relationship Riding philosophy to include personal issues such as low self-esteem and anger management. Barbra-Ann also offers private consultations through a one-on-one progressive program, allowing participants to explore their inner-self and pin point what is preventing them from attaining their goals in life.

Barbra-Ann also has a corporate background as a facilitator and does various speaking engagements.

For more information, visit www.relationshipriding.com